IDLER

THE ART OF LIVING · JULY—AUGUST 2018

libertas per cultum

IDLE LTD.
NO.61

Contents *Idler* No 61, July – August 2018

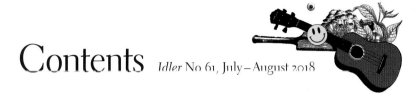

NOTES FROM THE COUCH

Readers' Letters   6

Idler's Diary   15

How I live
Aschlin Ditta: From standup
to screenwriter   18

Problems
With Virginia Ironside   22

Idler News
Andrew Smart howls at the
bullshit job of data science   24

Modern Toss   29, 39

The Good Stuff
Annabel Sampson and Charlotte
Brook enjoy the service of some
Fatbellypots, Naturist Cleaners,
a mobile cinema, Serial Box
and Oddbox   30

Technology
Harry R Lloyd on two delightful
devices that aim to slow
down time …   40

Poetry
with Murray Lachlan Young   44

FEATURES

Interview: Adam Curtis
Tom Hodgkinson gets the lowdown
on politics in the age of the
man-machine from TV's greatest
documentary journalist   51

Interview: Michael Pollan
Meet the psychedelics guru
who advocates hallucinogens
as therapy   65

Psycho weeds
Alice Smith's illustrations of
mind-bending plants   72

The lethargic pageant
The joys of cricket by Joe Mellen   81

Frying tonight
Cosmic necklaces, acid
T-shirts, dresses with doodles:
psychedelic fashion is back!   88

IDLE PURSUITS

Idle home
Joanne Brierley on how she
kitted out her Camberwell
cottage for coppers   93

CONTENTS

Art flâneur
Tim Richardson finds a gem
of a gallery in Surrey   101

Books
Cathleen Mair rounds up the
latest political thinking   108

Small press
David Collard sneers at the
supposed death of the novel   113

Craft
Ros Badger is inspired by
some botanical beauties   117

Music
Erland Cooper communes
with peregrine falcons to keep
Orkney on his mind   120

Jonnie Bayfield puts his head
on the block for the love of
malcontent Morrissey   123

Television
Kate Bernard on the fine art
of comedy   126

Astronomy
Robert Katz is searching the
heavens for the Goddess of Love   128

Travel
Tim Lott takes a
steampunk safari   132

Wine
Anne McHale meets the
hairdresser who turned to drink   138

Gin
Geraldine Coates takes a trip
around the country's premier
distilleries   141

Recipe
Victoria Hull provides a cheap
and tasty alternative to milk   144

Gardening
Graham Burnett talks us through
the healing properties of herbs   146

Beekeeping
How to make a cornershop for
your bees, by Bill Anderson   149

Snooker
Alex Johnson explains what
snooker commentators are going
on about   152

Escape
Like rust itself, management speak
never sleeps. Robert Wringham
plugs in the pacifier   154

Sheds
Alex Johnson is really moved by
the sheds that do not stay static   157

Eating out
Victoria Hull says *no* to private
members clubs and *yes* to the
traditional rub-a-dub   160

Beer
Evil Gordon casts some stellar
ales in leading roles   164

Ukulele
Cameron Murray meets the
King of Strings   168

Will Hodgkinson and Danny
Wootton get all fuzzy with
Felt frontman Lawrence   170

Idler questionnaire
The award-winning Ali Smith on
her passage from Littlewoods to
Man Booker   172

Idler is a bi-monthly published by Idle Ltd.,
Great Western Studios, 65 Alfred Road, London w2 5EU Tel: 0203 176 7907 idler.co.uk

Editor: Tom Hodgkinson
Art Director: Alice Smith
Sub-editors: Cathi Unsworth,
  Virginia Ironside
Typesetter: Christian Brett, Bracketpress
Programming Director: Victoria Hull
Marketing and editorial assistant:
  Cathleen Mair
Poetry Editor: Clare Pollard
Advisor: James Pembroke

Advertising:
Lisa Martin at Portman Media on
020 3859 7093 or lisa@portmanmedia.com

Copyright ©Idle Ltd. 2018
All rights reserved.
Idle Limited Reg. No.5897340
To subscribe go to: idler.co.uk/join

Printed and bound in the UK by Mixam
ISSN 1351-5098

Cover illustration by Alice Smith

Illustrations throughout the *Idler* (except where noted) by Alice Smith
alice-smith.co.uk twitter.com/asmithys instagram.com/aliceshole

Contributors: Aschlin Ditta, Virginia Ironside, Andrew Smart, Annabel Sampson, Charlotte
Brook, Harry R Lloyd, Murray Lachlan Young, Joe Mellen, Joanne Brierley, Tim Richardson,
David Collard, Ros Badger, Jonnie Bayfield, Kate Bernard, Tim Lott, Anne McHale, Geraldine
Coates, Graham Burnett, Bill Anderson, Alex Johnson, Robert Wringham, Evil Gordon,
Cameron Murray, Will Hodgkinson

Letter from the Editor

Dear Idlers,

It was a huge pleasure to spend some time with Adam Curtis for this issue. You are no doubt familiar with his work: from *The Century of the Self* to *Hypernormalisation*, Curtis has consistently uncovered fascinating stories around the movements of power in the 20th century. He is constantly questioning and constantly counter-intuitive, and refuses to toe the party line. For example: "People say there is a lot of information on the Internet. In fact there is very little." He also reveals the secret of his research techniques: "I read books."

I also went to see author Michael Pollan, the mushroom man, who has written a terrific book about psychedelic drugs and their therapeutic potential. For Pollan, a properly guided psilocybin trip can be immensely beneficial to your mental health and happiness, because of the way it can free you from the prison of the ego. We look forward to researching this subject further.

Elsewhere we are delighted to feature novelist Ali Smith and Joe Mellen on the joys of cricket – an idle pastime if ever there was one, either as participant or viewer.

Here's hoping for a long, hot psychedelic summer.

Peace,

Tom x

PS Please write to me at mail@idler.co.uk

Tom turns 50 in Italy [Photo: Chris Floyd]

Readers' Letters

Write to us at Great Western Studios, 65 Alfred Road, London W2 5EU *or email* mail@idler.co.uk. *Star letter wins an* Idler *tote bag*

Mission: Impossible

Sir: Have you ever tried to close an Amazon account? Having read the piece in *The Guardian* about Amazon's world dominance, I decided to cancel Prime and close my account. It's hilariously difficult. To start with, there is no option on the site that easily enables you to do this.

First, you have to find the "Contact us" page, accessible only through a separate web search, and start a web chat with an Amazon bot. When you ask to close your account, the bot asks you why. You tell them and they ask if you are sure and aware of the disastrous consequences to your life.

The bot sends you an email, which contains a long list of reasons not to close your account. You then click on a link and send another email requesting that your account be closed and all data deleted.

I managed to achieve all this only an hour ago – and currently my account is still there, nothing has happened and I just got a marketing email from Amazon.

How do we escape?

Ben Vonberg-Clark, by email

Run, salmon, run

Sir: While perusing your article "Two men in a pod" [*Idler* 59] I was surprised to read the phrase: "a group of salmon". For someone who writes regularly, and well, this seemed somewhat lazy as I am sure you would have imagined that a collective noun for salmon exists. In fact there are several depending on the situation. In this case it would be a "run" of salmon, "run" being the collective noun for salmon heading upriver to spawn. As well as having perhaps the least idle of all collective nouns, salmon are surely one of the least idle of all beings, travelling thousands of miles to their home river where they head upstream, without feeding, to spawn and probably die.

Declan Morrison, by email

Road to recovery

Sir: I have been on a personal journey after a serious health incident, following which I have had to relearn how to walk, pick things up, stand, use escalators, climb stairs on moving buses and cycle. My balance is still very poor and I move slowly so I am very aware of any changes in level, trip hazards, timing of crossings …

I have discovered an excellent way to get around, a Christiania cargo trike, that means I am now car-free. This was recommended by a Danish neurophysiologist, and is a normal part of Danish rehabilitation, but seems to be as rare as hen's teeth in the UK.

I am no longer safe to drive and have learned that car dependency is not needed. I get exercise, my trike carries stuff and it is a vehicle. I am involved with the charity Wheels for Wellbeing and would commend this "tool for conviviality" to enable life between buildings and as a key part of the idler utopia which is slowly being mapped.

Clive Durdle, by email

Tech-tonic

Sir: Young people don't know how to be idle. They understand doing little or nothing as something to be despised and rejected, rather than to be sought after and cherished. They feel a need to be online and in touch rather than offline and reflective. It is a sad state of affairs. When teens were asked to take themselves off the connection-grid for just a week, a recent study found that it was a real and substantial challenge – some even found the prospect of disconnecting so disturbing that they sought counselling advice before embarking on "such a major challenge". They discovered that taking a break from social media gave them a chance to spend more time with friends and family, get their homework done well in advance, "think deep thoughts", and spend more time outside. Some even found time for hobbies and to be creative. They found that being idle and bored were among the most creative and productive parts of their day.

Parents are not innocent bystanders. A friend sent us an invitation for dinner which read: "We are having friends round to stare at their phones and eat – maybe you would like to join them!" There are many families in which children compete with smartphones for their parents' attention.

It would be easy to see this as a personal issue which affects some young people and their families, but it affects us all. Since 1950 researchers have collected data about the Creativity Quotient of young people – a kind of IQ measure for creativity. Between 1950 and 1990 the CQ, as it is known, gradually rose alongside rises in IQ. But since then, it has steadily fallen, especially in the US. As CQ declines, so does our inventiveness, ability to respond to threat and challenge and the opportunity to create new and imaginative products, services and experiences. We all need our young people to be more creative rather than less, but many are becoming pessimistic. Technology discourages idleness because we seem to think the world demands our attention. It discourages creativity and the opportunity to use idleness to trigger imagination, passion and fun. We should all purge ourselves of a dependency on technology and return to simple pleasures and seek out idle time. It will not only help our well-being and health, but it will spur us to new things, like playing the banjo.
Stephen Murgatroyd,
PhD, by email

Napster

With her face framed by tumbling tresses, I was lost to her soothing, her tender caresses.

Miss Haylot would sing me away off to kip, as her fingers slipped through my Mowgli-straight hair, weaving songs with her breath out of whimsies, warm afternoon air. Now as an adult it doesn't seem fair, to be stuck in a puritan cult.

Afternoon naps should be back by demand. All the workers could drift off to doze with a smile. All the programs and the projects would get better planned, and the progress improved by an elegant mile.

Our effectiveness levels would soar, our desires to strive would improve and thrive.

We would be less likely to quit or move to competitor firms with a "No Napping" policy!

The economy wouldn't collapse. I would definitely change my career to a snoozing and napping overseer. Plumping down pillows, pouring camomile teas, covering cold elbows and errant knees with cashmere blankets.

It's a truth, we've only got ourselves to please. More akin to the Celts or the Swedes than the God-fearing Yanks or the sweatshop Chinese.

John Watson, by email

Sleeping Cats

Kevin

Owner: Phillipa Perry

Wake up! Time to die!

Sir: This morning I woke up and looked at my iPhone. A message read: "Don't forget you're going to die."

I have a new app called "WeCroak". It reminds me five times a day I'm going to die. In Bhutan they say contemplating death five times daily brings happiness. This app reminds me beautifully: "Don't forget you're going to die" – followed by a quote relating to death. Today's first quote: "How fine the mesh of death. You can almost see through it." This reminder of my death has replaced my husband's greeting: "Morning, beautiful!" I like veracity in the morning. The app's more credible than my husband's declaration.

WeCroak was number one on the Apple Store's health and fitness section. Its popularity is not surprising: contemplating mortality helps spur needed change. By reminding us of our finitude, we become aware of the freedom we have to direct our own lives.

On day four of having the app, I started to act recklessly. I've always wanted to go to Chicago, so I booked a ticket. I'm going on my own. I'm leaving everything behind. I deserve this.

It's not just reckless abandon that has taken hold of me; the app has stripped down a layer of my social angst. I always apologise when someone bumps into me, and because I'm afraid of offending anyone, I answer calls when I should be writing. Since having the app I feel braver and bolder. I realise that I'm both the monkey and the organ grinder of my own life.

In our heavily filtered world that's hell-bent on distorting reality, this app speaks the truth. It doesn't matter if I look fat today or if I've won the lottery, it doesn't care, it only has one response: "Don't forget you're going to die."

It has reminded me of my freedom and singularity in the world. My funeral may be attended by many, but my actual death will be a singular event belonging only to me. But there's no anguish in the face of my unlimited freedom. I'm off to Chicago.

Kiran Sidhu @KiranSidhu41

Something to vegetate on

Sir: I was inspired to write to you after reading Virginia Ironside's response to the woman who was worried about her daughter's desire to try veganism [*Idler* 60]. This letter is not intended as a rebuttal, merely an opportunity to put forward a case for what is so often seen as a joyless,

Readers' Loaves

Organic rye sourdough loaf
by David Hamblett

puritanical lifestyle – veganism.

1. As idlers, we strive for the good life. It does not make sense to be complicit in inflicting upon billions of farm animals the nasty, brutish and short lives we ourselves seek to avoid. Similarly, we seek to avoid the drudgery of wage slavery. It does not seem right to support the relentless, intensive exploitation of laying hens and dairy cows.

2. In my experience, veganism is compatible with good living. I have eaten a wider, more vibrant variety of food than at any prior point in my life. I also feel healthier and fitter, allowing me to better pursue my interests and hobbies.

3. There is a persistent myth that veganism is somehow expensive, elitist and unattainable to the common man. As with any diet, it can be as lavish or humble as your tastes dictate. Rice, beans and vegetables should be well within any budget – particularly tinned or frozen versions.

4. I find a certain ascetic clarity in eating relatively simply, which goes some way in reducing the tyranny of choice so prevalent in our modern economy of distraction and fleeting fancies.

5. I do not deny that many idlers take profound pleasure in succulent cuts of meat and pongy cheeses, but is your own brief enjoyment really worth as much as the whole life of a fellow creature?

6. Lakes of pungent, polluting faeces. Billowing clouds of methane. Intensive land and water usage. Complex and fragile ocean ecosystems dredged and left for dead. We are allowing the powerful, corporate busybodies to pillage our common resources, in the name of their own short-term profiteering. The biggest thing we can do to help preserve our planet for future generations is to take the leap and go vegan.

I hope this may give your readers food for thought. Now, pass me the hummus.

Stephen Gowie, Inverness

Nice work

Sir: I found myself in a bullshit job a while back [see David Graeber interview, *Idler* 60]. After a few years of avoiding work – busking, playing in bands and generally having fun – I decided to go back to university and do an MSc in Computing, figuring it was probably time to be an adult and there was good money to be earnt in the dot com boom (remember that?). I subsequently found myself as a graduate recruit in a large Telecoms Company. My bullshit job title was "Solution Designer".

I like to think I must have done

some useful stuff, but my heart really wasn't in it. I never got used to the weirdness of corporate life – the constant '"initiatives", the inefficiency, the waste, the TLAs (Three Letter Acronyms) and the general bullshit – but I took full advantage of their progressive family-friendly policies, such as working from home and part-time hours. I dropped my hours to spend some quality time with my guitars (and my children) but it was clear that if you wanted to go further in your "career" then you'd have to sell your soul 100%.

Three specific memories:

1. Breaking into fits of giggles when my line manager asked me with a straight face what I had been doing recently to "enhance shareholder value".
2. The time I opined to some colleagues that I was intending to apply for promotion so I could afford to work one less day for the same salary. Literally nobody understood where I was coming from.
3. Discovering that most of my senior colleagues were divorced because of the pressures of the job – so all the money they earnt was now paying for two mortgages which they worked 70–80 hour weeks to maintain.

It became obvious I was in the wrong job and so I took advantage of a fairly generous redundancy package. I found a nice part-time job in the not-for-profit world doing useful things (I hope) and although I think four days a week still tips the balance in favour of work, for the moment it suits me well. The moment I can afford to drop another day's work in favour of home, I will. Keep up the good work.

Chris Walker, Cardiff

Peterson defended

Sir: I just watched the first couple of clips from your online course "How to fix the future". In your opening remarks, you use the words "freedom", "autonomy" and "control". With an added dash of irreverent *joie de vivre*, I think these concepts sum up the underlying philosophy of the *Idler*.

Therefore, I'm bemused by the rather throw-away criticism of Jordan Peterson's 12 *Rules for Life* [*Idler* 60].

Firstly, the book certainly does not teach you "how to be a complete arsehole". In fact, it is entirely in keeping with the *Idler* philosophy of achieving greater autonomy and freedom. For me, it came as a philosophical breath of fresh air.

It appears that whoever wrote the article has simply read the chapter titles and dismissed the book based on those. If you have read it, and decided it's complete bullshit, then that's fine and I'll just disagree with you. However, if the article is based on an incorrect premise by someone who hasn't read the book, then shame on you, especially if it discourages others from reading it.

Even if you disagree with some of the ideas, I think Jordan Peterson's book is one of the most important to be written in recent years. The chapter titles are actually spoofs, with the content offering deep and insightful observations on some important issues.

The chapter entitled "Set your own house in perfect order before you criticise the world" is an essay on the nature and dangers of religious and political fundamentalism, and not "terribly hard work and unrealistic", as you suggest.

12 *Rules for Life* is not a "self-help" book even if the title implies otherwise. The book is worthy of a read, and deserves serious and thoughtful criticism in the *Idler* rather than a piss-take.

I rather hope that the "ambitious young clerks" you mention do read the book. If they do, they might get some useful ideas on how to form an escape committee and start digging a tunnel.

Phillip Tanswell, by email

Kerosene conspiracy

Sir: In April, you wrote of an idyllic birthday break at a villa in Italy. Similarly, the *Idler* sometimes invites supporters to be part of events that take place in Italy. In neither of these is there any sense that getting to these locations might cause suffering for others, via the burning of untaxed kerosene in the planes that I imagine most participants would be choosing as their favoured mode of transport. That kerosene has been produced at a massive, painful cost to communities unfortunate enough to live near oil fields and refineries. And that's without beginning to factor in the suffering that fossil fuel-triggered climate change is bringing – and will bring – to untold members of all plant and animal species on this wondrously beautiful and diverse planet. So, to boil it down: I hope that a core part of the *Idler* mantra is that idling should nonetheless have a moral code based on kindness to oneself and to all and sundry – that it ought to be a fantastic, less destructive way of living than contant busyness. If that's the case, then surely carbon-heavy idle pursuits contradict that core ethos? And if so, might the *Idler* reconsider promoting the use of planes to reach higher states of idlery?

Mark Brown, by email 🐌

Idler's diary
Ramblings around town

Send your stories to us at mail@idler.co.uk

Is idleness the new hygge?

This summer sees the release of a veritable rash of books advocating idling, slowing down, wasting time and all the rest of it. *In Praise of Wasting Time* by novelist Alan Lightman has a nice title but the insides, sadly, do not live up to its promise. It is based on a TED talk, and like most products of the TED empire, dresses up platitudinous observations – "wouldn't it be great if we all just ... slowed down a little bit?" – as inspiring philosophical breakthroughs. He uses the phrase "hyper-connected world" about 15 times and we see the familiar old tales about Einstein wandering about thinking and so on. *Idleness* by Brian O'Connor is not so much an "idle lifestyle" book as a serious academic study of idleness, bunging in vast dollops of Kant and Hegel, the ur-philosophers. It is worth ploughing through as he has unearthed some very interesting material, particularly from Robert Burton's *Anatomy of Melancholy*, which advised the depressives of the 17th century: "Be not solitary, be not idle." Dr Johnson adapted that to: "When solitary, be not idle; when idle, be not solitary." Then there is *On Doing Nothing: Finding Inspiration in Idleness* by an illustrator called Roman Muradov which we have not yet seen but whose cover looks quite charming. Is there a ... movement afoot?

Reader revolt

The news that British Telecom announced the shedding of 13,000 jobs in management led *Idler* editor Tom Hodgkinson to theme his weekly newsletter around the idea of bullshit jobs, the title of David Graeber's excellent new polemic. "Maybe we should be rejoicing rather than gnashing our teeth and wailing with despondency?" he suggested. "Maybe these corporate slaves will now taste sweet freedom, and run into the woods and dance

15

round the maypole!" Alas, many readers did not see the funny or positive side. "Free to run to the food banks more like!" said John Harris of the *Guardian*. "Seriously? You think people losing their jobs is funny?!" said Fi Glover of the BBC. And others wrote to say: "It is all very well for you and your Hooray Henry chums, strumming your ukuleles in Hampstead, with all your privilege. Some people have to feed their families ... your message shows an astonishing myopia. Cancel my subscription!"
Could these correspondents not see that this was a message of hope?

Booze news
Thanks to Mark Forsyth for entertaining us all at May's *Idler* Dinner with tales from his book, *A Short History of Drunkenness.*

"The Egyptians were great binge drinkers. At one particular festival it was necessary to drink until you vomited – the vomiting was very important – then drink again until you vomited, then again and again. After this, there'd be an enormous orgy – which must have been very unpleasant, considering all the vomit. You'd think accidental pregnancies wouldn't be much of a worry after all that drinking, so it was considered a great honour to be conceived at the orgy. Any child conceived there received an immediate priesthood when born.

"The Aztecs were very disapproving of drunkenness, but when they did indulge at festivals they worked on the 400 rabbit system. This is because 400 rabbits were said to be the sacred children of the goddess of alcohol, and how many rabbits signified how drunk you were – e.g. if you were 10 rabbits, you were mildly tipsy, etc. Public drunkenness was illegal and punished by public strangulation, except for the nobility who would be strangled in private. Though the prohibition on drunkenness was only for the young, it being thought the elderly had learnt how to handle themselves ..."

Psych kicks
Thanks to French pop geniuses Gloria for playing at the *Idler* Party at Bush Hall in the spring. It's difficult to avoid clichés when describing pop music but their Byrds-tinged girl psych-pop harmonies won over the crowd. Keep a lookout for them – buy their vinyl – dig their style.

More sleep and less work for better mental health
A charity called Mental Health UK reckons that six in ten people wake up suddenly in the night worrying about work. That's according to a poll of 2,000 people carried out with a manufacturer of mattresses. At the same time, we notice that fat

cat's newspaper the *Financial Times* has run a "sleep" supplement as clearly workers in what is called the "financial sector", i.e. the money lenders, are not getting enough. The remedy, it would seem, is more sleep and less work. So it's official: idleness is good for you.

Eno gets idle

An interview with ambient pioneer Brian Eno, where he advises young people to avoid getting a job, has been viewed over a quarter of a million times on YouTube.
Mr Eno's advice is surely very sensible as work worries are the cause of sleeplessness and mental health issues, as are a lack of creativity and autonomy in daily life.

Anti-social network

The computer scientist Jaron Lanier reckons that social media, by its nature, makes you into an arsehole. It encourages arseholey behaviour by rewarding it with more notifications, engagements and all of the rest of it. His new book, discussed at a recent *Idler* evening with the *Guardian*'s John Harris, is called *Ten Reasons Why You Should Delete Your Social Media Accounts Now.* ☺

Thanks to David Oldroyd-Bolt

How I live

Aschlin Ditta:
From standup to screenwriter…

… and back again. How a diary entry turned one man's life in the opposite direction

The other day I found my diary from the last standup gig I did 23 years ago, and read these words: "Listen, if I get to 50 and my life has turned to shit, I promise myself now that I will do another gig."

So, ladies and gentlemen …
It's nice to be back.

As the sweat poured down my neck and my heart reached a pace that it had never achieved through exercise, I'd delivered the first joke on stage in over two decades and it got a laugh. Not a massive one, but enough for me to go on and tell my next gag and indeed a few more to fill my allotted five minutes. I managed to cover a variety of topics, from how men of my age tend not to be jihadis due to their dwindling interest in sleeping with virgins, to whether, looking back, I really did remember to mention to my partner we were in an open relationship. It was hardly cutting edge but it was a start.

The reason all of this nonsense is happening in my life is that the opening line of that joke is actually true: I did find my diary, it did say that and I'm pretty sure my life could be going a whole lot better.

As a screenwriter and an Arsenal fan, most of my life is spent waiting for something to happen, and for a good portion of that time I'm standing in queues at my local Co-op. Instead of writing, I'm usually wondering what the hell I should eat that will allow me to look more like a moderately successful writer and less like a fat mess, although they are of course usually the same thing. Will I keep the kale and salad that's filling my basket or will I just put everything back on the shelves and go next door for a tuna mayonnaise baguette? That. I'll do that. I always do that. But the continued delusion

Aschlin not being the foundation of the film industry

that one day I might not is the most exciting part of my day as a working screenwriter.

The first thing you have to know about being a screenwriter is this: if you can make a living, it's a great way to make one. The second thing you have to know is that you're probably not going to make a living. The third thing is that even if you do, the industry is not about you. It has never been about you and it never will be about you. The last thing you have to know is that they will tell you that it is about you. They'll tell you it's all about you. You will hear things like: "You can make a great script into a bad movie

but you can never make a bad script into a great movie." You'll hear things like: "Film is about script, script and script, we would have nothing to say if it were not for the script." It's wonderful to know that, as a screenwriter, you are the foundation stone of the entire film and television industries.

Unfortunately it's not true. Film is about the Director; television is about the Producer; and both are all about the Actors. And none of those are you! Remember, if it were about you then maybe the public could name more than one screenwriter, instead of none. Jesus, I am a screenwriter and I can only name three, and one of them is my writing partner … and one of them is me. Two, I can name two.

So, having explained the low grade misery that is succeeding in one's chosen profession, why did I decide after 20 years to get back on the stage to try to make people laugh? Well, I am about to turn 50, that's just a fact, and about three months ago I was in said Co-op queue when, just at the moment at which I was about to break my daily delusion and put back the ingredients for a Greek salad with kale, I witnessed an event that brought everything into focus.

In front of me stood a couple, possibly in their early twenties, it was hard to tell. They were pushing and shoving one another in the beer aisle, laughing, discussing what to drink, what colour Rizlas to buy. They laughed that laugh, the one that feels real, a genuine reaction to a genuine moment. Not the laugh I'm dealing in these days, the laugh that is forced out, a conspiratorial noise that allows the awfulness of middle age to be spread among only those ready to hear it. No, their laughs were different, and just as the girl turned to her boyfriend and almost lifted him off the floor with one single, intense kiss on the lips, a thought landed in the middle of my head like a cluster bomb in a built-up area: these two people would be having more excitement in the next 12 hours of their lives than I would be in the next 12 years.

I was devastated, truly devastated, and even the tuna mayonnaise baguette next door had lost its appeal. I'd had an actual realisation; a moment of truth. Any kind of fun that may once have been on the cards had gone. There were no cards, there were just memories, memories of a life I'd lived, or I'd hoped I'd lived, or assumed I'd lived.

Something had to change. I remembered the diary entry and concluded that the only thing that would frighten me enough into actually feeling something again would be to go back to the standup. I needed to deal with real people again, not just people trying to hang on to their jobs. I wanted to connect again, to put myself on the line without the protection of a laptop and a WiFi connection.

I set about calling around the old haunts, like the King's Head, Crouch End, where I had done my very first pun-based open spot in 1994, and Up The Creek, a terrifying gig that I had played a lot and had achieved three times as many offers of violence as I had laughs. Then there was the Comedy Brewhouse in Islington, a venue that offered me a gig for life due to the fact I once went on stage drunk, did three minutes of

Is Aschlin the new Lenny Bruce?

material to a packed audience, then passed out and fell off the stage resulting in a huge laugh and 20 stitches in my face.

I settled on a small gig in Covent Garden and off I went, armed with some anecdotes about letting people down and truths about being generally hopeless. It was very strange to go back into a pub not just to drink and talk but to entertain, and if my sole aim was to scare myself into feeling again then it was surely achieved.

I felt the terror of hearing my name announced by the MC who they loved. I felt the heat of the spotlight that immediately dries the mouth and the brain. I felt the judgement of the half-cut punters who might have wanted me to be funny but might just enjoy it more

if I wasn't. Would I remember that opening line? Did I have any others to follow it? Well somehow I did. The fear, the pain and the anxiety was back … and I loved it.

I don't know whether I'll carry on or not, indeed whether anyone will ever book me again, but I do know this, I'm done with the waiting and I'm done with the tuna baguettes. After all, as an old comedian once said to me: "I'd rather be a terrible comic than great at anything else."

I've certainly achieved the first part, now let's see about the next.

Aschlin Ditta's film Swimming With Men *is released in cinemas nationwide on 6 July. His book* Things I Wrote While I Should Have Been Writing *is sitting on his desktop waiting to find the courage of its convictions.*

21

Problems

Virginia Ironside

Our agony aunt tells it straight. Send your issues to us at mail@idler.co.uk

Anxiety attack

My son of 12, who up till now has been a happy and sociable boy, has suddenly, in the last six weeks, got extremely worried about war. He wakes with nightmares about nerve gas, and rings me twice a day from school panicking about the possibility of nuclear war if North Korea ever decide to attack us. He's OK for a while and then suddenly gets overwhelmed by these fears. I have asked the school what they think and they suggest he sees a psychiatrist. My husband is reluctant to go down this route but I am desperate to help him. What do you think?

Antonia

AROUND this age my own son got into a terrible panic about the idea of war. Apparently it is an extremely common anxiety at this age, particularly with boys, who can suffer with what's known as "separation anxiety". Suddenly they realise that they are growing up and will have, at some point, to leave home. This prospect – probably entirely subconscious – can be absolutely terrifying.

My own feeling is that for the moment you should keep your nerve. Your husband can probably intuitively read the mind of a boy of this age better than you – and six weeks is a bit early to start taking drastic action like seeing a psychiatrist. Once you go down that route you'll probably get into a cycle of pills or, worse, therapy, and start to medicalise what is an entirely normal stage of your son's life. You'll make him feel odd – the last thing he needs to feel at the moment.

I'd wait a month or even two and only then, if it appears to be getting unbearable for the poor chap, think of getting professional help. In the meantime, just be there for him, reassure him and don't go away and leave him, even with sympathetic grandparents or friends, for any length of time, because this will make things worse for him.

Enough already

I've got a good job, a nice flat, a car and my children go to good state schools. We live reasonably well and don't want for anything. But two of my friends who I was at school with are worrying me because one of them works all hours of the day and has just bought a racehorse, while another has bought his third house in two years – he doesn't need it because he'll only stay there occasionally. I was wondering: what it is that drives some people just to go on and on wanting to make money? Are they never satisfied?

Judes

You – and I incidentally – are very fortunate that we're not driven by a desire to accumulate. This desperation to make more and more money is probably a sign of grandiosity, suffered, usually, by people who feel, at heart, very small indeed. Accumulation of wealth assuages the feeling temporarily until they're driven to buy even more stuff. Eventually, they'll only be able to move with other people also driven by greed and once they're in that circle they'll find it difficult to get out of. Thank your lucky stars that the good fairy at your christening gave you the gift of knowing that enough is enough.

Death duty

My father died a few months ago and although we didn't let our children come to the funeral – they are four and five and he was a much-loved grandfather – we are wondering whether it's a good idea to let them come to the memorial service? I know they will be terribly upset and not only do I not want to distress them, I don't want them to take away from the whole event by being obviously unhappy.

Christine

I THINK it was a great mistake not to encourage them to come to the funeral. Children are much more sensible about things like funerals than adults and although they may be temporarily upset, a funeral at any age won't do them nearly as much harm as if this whole important ritual is kept from them. You're lucky – you've got a second chance. The memorial service will be an opportunity for them not only to feel sad but also realise what a tip-top chap their grandfather was and to feel pride in him as well as sorrow for his death. Who cares if they cry… no one will mind and I'm sure they'll be able to handle it. 🐚

Idler News

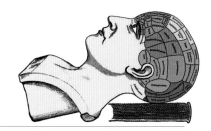

By Andrew Smart

Brain drain
Why are all the clever people being sucked into advertising sales scams?

The hottest neologism in Silicon Valley and increasingly the rest of the economy is data science. Every year, thousands of newly-minted Masters and PhDs in data science flock to Silicon Valley hoping to land jobs at the valley's heavy-hitters, like Apple, Google or Facebook, as data scientists. Physicists, chemists, computational biologists who have spent a decade toiling away and getting emotionally abused in graduate school only to emerge on the desert called the academic job market are forced to enter industry as … wait for it … data scientists. Entry level salaries for data scientists in tech are in six figures. There are perks like free food, restricted stock units, ping pong tables and sofas in the office. These benefits are often too

much to resist in comparison to an indefinite post-doctoral time of financial instability, cutthroat competition and uncertainty in academia. All those computational skills you might learn as a biology PhD, studying the mysteries of protein-folding in tumours that might one day save lives, can now be put to good use by targeting ads on Facebook.

On Twitter, the tech futurist Mark Pesce altered Alan Ginsberg's *Howl* to reflect the current situation with data science:

I SAW THE GREATEST MINDS OF MY
GENERATION
STARVING
HYSTERICAL
NAKED
USING THEIR PHDS TO DELIVER

MORE TARGETED ADVERTISING TO AN
EVER-SHRINKING AUDIENCE OF
EVER-RICHER FOLKS

But what is it that *makes* data science a science? Simply because we attach the word science to the word data? What about Christian Science? Or Political Science? A common answer to the question of what makes science science is: to understand, explain and predict the world. The purpose of data science is then to understand, explain and predict … data? Developing a philosophy of data science would allow us to probe deeper and ask questions that data scientists do not themselves ask. For example, we should identify implicit assumptions in data science practice which data scientists do not explicitly discuss – these can be ontological: what kind of objects are data? Epistemological: how do we know about them? And ethical: what and whose values do we or should data scientists use?

Of course the answer about what makes a science a bona fide science is tricky, which is why we have the much maligned discipline of "philosophy of science". Philosophy of science asks those difficult and unresolvable questions: What is objectivity? Why and how does science make progress? *Does* science make progress? Toward what? Is the universe physically comprehensible? What and whose values should science use in judging scientific knowledge? But we do not have anything like philosophy of data science. What would a philosophy of data science look like?

First we might try to answer what data science purports to study: data. What is data? The word data is the plural form of *datum* – a mostly depreciated word. Pedantic scientists gleefully remind people that the word "data" should take the plural verb "are" instead of "is" – as in, "the data are good". But of course language changes fast and the word "data" is now most naturally singular.

But what *are* data, really? Shouldn't this be the question data science is concerned with rather than predicting "time to click" on some button in a mobile app? More philosophically, Jonathan Furner asks, "What, precisely, are data? Of what kind (or genus) of thing are they? Under what conditions can something count as a datum? What properties must something have if it is to be, or perhaps to play the role of, a datum?" Or you might want to be able to say something like: "X are data if and only if X are …."

The *Oxford Dictionary of Statistics* defines data as: "Information, usually numerical or categorical." But this quickly becomes a tautology: information is data if and only if it is information, usually numerical or categorical. So how would data scientists answer the question, what properties do all and only instances of data have in common with one another?

Indeed most people – data scientists included – might intuitively define data to be some kind of information. This raises the complex question: what is information? There does exist a rich discipline called "philosophy of information" which tries to tackle this question. A philosophy of data science would try to understand what data scientists are *really* doing often without their awareness.

Physics, biology and chemistry each want to reveal the secrets of nature – they collect data to answer specific questions about nature. Social science tries to understand how society works. Psychology wants to understand the mind, neuroscience the brain. But what is the big secret about data that data science is trying to reveal? What are the general theories of data that explain the phenomena of data? Are there laws of data like there are laws of physics? Moreover, what exactly are the phenomena a data scientist is studying? Clicks? Page views? In my experience, these kinds of questions will often get you

annoyed blank stares at most tech companies.

Because data science is a young discipline it might be forgiven for not having a clear scientific purpose. Science too has long been struggling with defining exactly what it is and what it is for. We are in the midst of a replication crisis in science and of course the integrity of science itself is undermined by the same market logic from which data science emerged. But in a nutshell what science is after is a meaningful understanding of the universe. Whether the ultimate nature of the universe is comprehensible to humans is still an ongoing debate in philosophy and physics.

If you can write Python or R scripts, have some understanding of SQL or Hadoop data structures and databases, and have an understanding of statistics and algorithms that goes beyond knowing what a distribution is, then you can reasonably call yourself a data scientist. These skills mean that you can query an enormous database, transform the results of that query into manageable structures, run statistics on the data, and finally create a model of what new data of a similar type will look like. But why would a data scientist want to do any of this? It's tedious, error-prone and often data scientists use off-the-shelf black-box algorithms they don't really understand themselves.

Most jobs in data science will require you to produce "actionable insights" and do it very fast. An example of an actionable insight from a data scientist might be to predict what is called "ad load" in a news feed – in other words how many ads at which frequency will users tolerate before they check out. Once you know this, the engineers at the company can make sure that users only see a certain number of ads. While this mundane triviality is fascinating to advertisers and social media companies for obvious reasons, is the accurate prediction of optimal ad load in a news feed scientifically interesting? Can one imagine a Nobel Prize for solving this mysterious puzzle? (Perhaps if Facebook starts to sponsor the prize.) Does predicting ad load seem like a worthwhile pursuit for a young PhD in physics? Ideally for a tech company a news feed would be nothing but ads, but then of course everyone would stop using the product so there would be nobody to see the ads. It is without question an interesting *engineering* challenge to accomplish this on the scale of hundreds of millions of users, but does this advance our understanding of anything – even data?

In other words what is ad load versus data about it? Is ad load something like the melting point of lead? We might take several measurements of the melting point of lead.

The late physicist David Bohm thought that prediction in science should not be the focus, "Indeed, in most cases, the content of what the research scientist predicts is *in itself* actually rather trivial (the precise paths of particles, the precise number of instruments that will register a certain phenomenon, and so forth). Unless there were something beyond this that could give it significance, this activity would be petty, and, indeed, even childish." Data scientists predict how many users will click on an ad, whether a ranking algorithm is increasing daily active minutes and so forth. The something beyond these trivial things is merely whether any of this leads to more money, and so much of data science remains petty and childish. Bohm points out that scientists feel a fundamental need to discover and create something new that is whole and total, harmonious and beautiful. In the tech world however the only harmonious and beautiful thing is more users using your produce more often.

It turns out that there are no answers to these philosophical questions about data science – at least not scientific ones. The vast majority of fancy data science models with a zillion hyperparamters are trying to do one thing only: getting you to use an app all day everyday to boost online advertising revenue. The "science" part of data science is no more than analysing the vast log data of millions of users and predicting what kinds of users are going to what and how can an algorithm be tweaked to get users to look at or click on this ad or that tab.

Data scientists spend their time organising and arranging enormous piles of data just so the data can begin to be analysed. The goal of data science seems to be not *understanding* but *control and manipulation*. It shares this dubious goal with other long discredited research areas like eugenics.

Eugenics did not want to understand anything new about humans, it wanted to judge what types of humans are better based on the false belief that there exist meaningful genetic differences among races, and that society could be improved by manipulating genes. Eugenics failed as a science because it was based on the ideologically motivated idea that we can judge the quality of human genes, and therefore determine what "good" humans are. Data science looks for patterns in data, but only patterns that assist the preconceived idea of profit – thus "good" data science is only

judged relative to whether it can make money.

The darker side of data science is the increasing use of algorithms to do what is called "predictive policing" where police reports from biased human police officers are fed into predictive algorithms. According to lead research scientist at Human Rights Data Group Kristian Lum, "Machine learning algorithms trained with data that encode human bias will reproduce, not eliminate, the bias."

Unsurprisingly, the algorithms tell the police officers to police black and Latino neighborhoods where they're already over-policing and thus generating more data from these neighborhoods. And this naturally leads to more arrests, which convinces the police that the algorithms are correct. This creates a tautological feedback loop from which we can only conclude that more policing of an area leads to more arrests – which should actually make the police department pause and reflect on its own biases. But the use of data science has the opposite effect. Data science is used as an "objective" measure to justify preexisting biases. What is scientific about reproducing institutional biases with maths?

Physicist Erwin Schrödinger wrote that, "The most careful record, if not inspected, tells us nothing." He was describing the strange paradox of objective knowledge and observation: even the results of the most painstaking and complicated experiments must still be subjectively *observed* by individual human scientists in order to be known. It is the same with the output of predictive algorithms and data science – someone with a specific background and specific values must observe the result and interpret within their own epistemological framework. This pernicious problem in philosophy of science is especially critical in data science where the output can be used to decide whether someone goes to jail, gets a job, gets a house or gets fired.

Modern Toss

The Good Stuff

Annabel Sampson *and* Charlotte Brook *are consciously consuming*

Full of character: Fatbellypots

Katherine Kingdom, a perfectly alliterative name that would make for a memorable byline, worked for years as a secondary school art teacher. She has only very recently reduced her working hours in order to pursue the ceramics that she makes in her garden shed. It was her brother who put her forward for the Good Stuff, with a side-note: "This is very much cottage level industry." Katherine's ceramic offering is two-pronged; she makes figures and vessels. The figures are ungainly and heroic. They're strange potato-headed creatures, sometimes with long legs and often with protruding bellies – true to the name Fatbellypots. They're an unlikely union between the Plasticine figure Morph, the spindly characters in *The Nightmare Before Christmas* and the creatures of Wes Anderson's imagination (think: *Fantastic Mr Fox* and *Isle of Dogs*). The vessels are equally eccentric: urns, pots and vases with figurative relief depicting more of these people. Across the relief, stories evolve. Katherine admits that she "enjoys the dynamics within a group". As do we. They're pots to make your imagination float.

fatbellypots.art

Skin deep: Naturist Cleaners

Mankind is at his most idle when dressed in his birthday suit. We were born that way, we take a bath that way and some of us even sleep that way. Some of our most indulgent, idle pursuits are done in the buff. That's why we think that Naturist Cleaners are a grand – albeit bold – idea, taking a hallmark of idleness and pasting it onto a quotidian task. Naturist Cleaners make an "experience" of your weekly clean (or so they say). This works two ways; they can either do your dusting starkers, or, they'll perform fully clothed and allow the customer to lounge leafless, buttocks bared.

You might think that this sounds like a seedy business – it's really not. The website looks like a Unilever product; all white, blue and sanitary. This is no underground operation. Also, quite happily, the nude cleaners pictured on the website come in all shapes and sizes. Real-looking women – fat, thin, warts and all – who, clearly, just enjoy a nude spring clean. "A sparkling clean home with cleaners who love what they do," is what their website promises. The *Idler* philosophy is rooted in fulfillment, so Naturist Cleaning is surprisingly spot on.

naturistcleaners.co.uk

Binge reading: Serial Box

Apart from all being written by Charles Dickens, what do *Nicholas Nickleby*, *Bleak House* and *David Copperfield* have in common? The answer is that they were all released as serials in the 1800s – that is, in monthly instalments. Literary giants like Elizabeth Gaskell and Anthony Trollope also dabbled in the genre. Technology – the "fourth industrial revolution" – and our social media-addled, 280-character-restricted attention spans have led to a happy revival of the format. Serial Box has been nicknamed "The HBO of reading" as old classics are rewritten in titbit form to induce binge-watching in book form: binge-reading.

How does it work? The serialised fiction is released in episodes each week, to electronic devices like a Kindle or iPad, with the option to read as chapters, listen as an audio book or flick between the two formats.

The current Serial Box library offers original commissions and old classics, restructured into 20-minute chunks. Parents may well approve of this kind of binging. This is an idle and enriching bed-bound alternative to back-to-back box sets. It's a format that's perfect for commutes and a preferable alternative to mindless scrolling through Instagram feeds. Get lost in 20 minutes of *Belgravia* by Julian Fellowes or the multi-authored *False Idols*, set in Cairo's glittering art world.

It costs subscribers about £1.15 to download each episode. Stories are generally stretched across 10–16 weeks.

serialbox.com

On the road: Vintage Mobile Cinema

Audrey would be a joy to pass by on the road. Spruced-up in old-fashioned cream and with her curved glass front, she looks like a slice of the Barbican's Botanical Conservatory, with the appealing words "Vintage Mobile Cinema" printed on her back door. Audrey is the sole survivor of a governmental vision of mobile cinemas thought up in the 1960s. They were built to travel around engineering firms and give training sessions to help increase productivity. After a successful pilot, more were made, but eventually sold off in 1974. Audrey is the only known survivor of the seven vehicles and has undergone a loving restoration project.

The Good Stuff came across her at the Edinburgh Fringe Festival in 2016, where she provided welcome shelter from the pervasive rain. Inside the gloriously upholstered 22-seater rouge and raked auditorium we watched early black-and-white footage of the fashionable crowds that first went to the Edinburgh Festival on its 70th anniversary.

This summer, Audrey will be appearing at the Contemporary Craft Festival, Tolpuddle Radical Film Festival and the Borders Books Festival among others. More listings, dates and Audrey's spot at the festivals are listed on her website.

vintagemobilecinema.co.uk

Urban woodland: Jim Bobart

With very cheerful illustrations of rabbits, moles and other woodland creatures flipping pancakes, strumming sitars and nibbling on cake, James Ward of Jim Bob Art is making quite a name for himself. But art like this – anthropomorphism, where animals are dressed up and take on human characteristics – is historically popular. Its protagonist, Sir Edwin Landseer (1802–73), was among the most admired of Victorian Britain. Audiences delighted in his *Laying down the*

Law with a poodle cast as the judge, his spectacles resting upon a book as he lectured the pups of the jury. If history informs the present, as it so often does, then hooray for Jim Bob. He also creates ceramic objects – mainly plates – with hand-painted captions to match the drawings; like greedy moles enquiring: "Are we having pancakes?" and a peckish racoon snacking on Ladurée: "Mr Racoon loves a macaroon!"

jimbobart.com

34

Veg out: Oddbox

It's a classic "Why did no one think of this before?" job – veg boxes stocked with produce that's been rejected by supermarkets for being too big, too small or too weird. Husband and wife Emilie Vanpoperinghe and Deepak Ravindran went from working at Deutsche Bank and a charity spin-off of the Nike Foundation respectively to start up Oddbox, an idea they had when they ate some delicious, freaky-shaped tomatoes at a Portugese market on holiday.

"When we got home we did some research and found out about 30% of British produce is turned away by shops because of tight specifications, or because it's surplus," Emilie told us. Oddbox is currently supplied by over 30 growers and delivers boxes of veg, fruit or a mix, either as a one-off or as a weekly subscription. Some stats: they give 10% of the produce to London charities and have so far saved 90 tons of groceries from hitting the compost heap. Excellently, because the veg are wacky-shaped, the boxes are about a third cheaper than a standard veg box. Cheap as chips – although they're not actually full of potatoes, the classic box-filling trick. Order this month and you'll get English strawberries from Kent, courgettes and curvy cucumbers, then plums and gourds in a couple of weeks. You're encouraged to keep your box and leave it out: they'll collect and re-use it. Currently delivering to south London, they hope to cover the whole capital within the next 12 months.

oddbox.co.uk

Elbow crease: 31 Chapel Lane

In spite of many nun-like qualities, the Good Stuff are not women of the cloth. We do, however, know a fine weave when we see one and when it's been sewn up to make a simple but rather chic item of clothing. Textile brand 31 Chapel Lane was founded by married couple Damien (a trained architect) and Joi (who has worked in law, health and social enterprise). From a converted Georgian building in Limerick, they design and make modern clothes and tea towels from fabrics – Donegal Tweed and Irish linen – woven on Ireland's dwindling number of surviving looms. Lovely shirts, but do you need to be very good at ironing to have one?

"Of course not!" we are told. Great. "About half the customers iron their garments, and half prefer naturally creased. We put ours through a 30°C wash, hang on coat hanger and leave it as is."

The bestseller is the Milana shirt – a white, basic take on an Elizabeth I ruff collar. The idea is that: "If you are getting dressed in the dark you would feel safe to walk out of your closet in this, even if it was inside out!" Future plans include working with Irish lace-makers and producing some hand-knitted kit for winter.

31chapellane.com

Leather for life: Craftory

While training to be an airline pilot, Estonian Mihkel Männik was working in a leather goods import company, but didn't like the punky, studded commercial stuff they were churning out. He discovered vegetable-tanned Swedish leather and started making minimalist purses from it in Tallinn, under the name Craftory, with the aim of being the "anti-Versace": a small craft company, making plain, simple goods.

He relocated to London in 2016, where he now has a leather-making team and studio in E8's Netil House. Plans for a market stall are in motion: until then, you can find the lusciously smooth honey-brown bi-fold *portmonnaies*, (that's wallets to us, Craftory's first and favourite product), rucksacks, belts and satchels at a range of retailers, from design store Bonds near London Fields to the Mayfair gentlemen's suitmakers Richard Gelding Ltd.

craftory.com

Frozen assets: Cool Box By Ruby

A box-fresh business purveying perhaps Britain's idlest, yet healthiest, hot dinners, By Ruby cooks, packs up and dispatches delicious and nutritious meals to order online. They have it delivered anywhere in the country and you cook it from frozen. Idyllic!

It's a partnership between Julia Bannister, Milly Bagot and Ruby Bell. Julia founded Finns, a shop, deli and catering company on Chelsea Green's sandwich-triangle of turf 30 years ago, which her niece Milly now co-runs and where Ruby used to be head chef. Having clocked shop customers bulk-buying casseroles to take home and freeze for future back-up, they saw a gap in the market between bad frozen meals and home-made, fresh deli food. By Ruby dishes cater for everyone, from meat-and-two-veg types to vegans, and there's a range of soups.

Ruby's sister Indigo is a graphic designer and helped with the website and glorious box designs. "Ruby was born in Mallorca, so we thought it would be fun to make the boxes look a bit like a tiled Mediterranean kitchen,'" she explained. Sturdy heifers and saddleback pigs, inspired by old butcher's shop signage were drawn by hand. On seeing it, the gobby Good Stuff hollered: "You should get it made into fabric!" Turns out they obviously already have. All packaging is recyclable and delivery cartons are insulated by 100% felted sheep's wool.

Refreshingly, in a London food-entrepreneur scene dominated by beards, brawn and vanilla-flavoured bloggers, By Ruby's three founders are very funny, very friendly, and all women. Ruby and co-chef Kasia cook everything from scratch in a rented kitchen in Acton equipped with a walk-in freezer, where they chop and sauté while grooving to Radio 2. Which dish would they turn to for an emergency date night? "Maybe the black bean chilli," Milly reckons. "Delicious with a dollop of guacamole, a few nachos and a cold lager."

byruby.co.uk

Modern Toss

Technology
Slow hand

Harry R Lloyd *on the Swiss watchmakers who aim to slow down time and the steampunk's answer to the smartphone*

THE Industrial Revolution radically changed our relationship with time. Before the 18th century, rough-and-ready methods of timekeeping – think sundials and Crocodile Dundee's hat – yoked our perception of time to the seasons. A daylight "hour" would drag on forever in the languid days of summer, but would fly by quick as a flash in the bleak winter months. The rise of shift work changed all that, creating an obsession for timing our work precisely by the chimes of the mechanical clock.

Now, the Swiss makers of the Slow Watch are trying to turn the tide against the worship of precision. In doing so, they hope to help us achieve a less hurried pace of life.

The Slow Watch is built to what its makers describe as a: "24-hour, one-hand concept". The watch face has neither minute nor second hand, and displays 24 hours rather than 12. This is designed to forestall the "unnatural" habit of splitting the day into two 12-hour halves. It also means that the finest-grained index markers measure in intervals of 15 minutes each. This will suit the idler right down to the ground. So much the better if your friend is 10 minutes late to meet you; that's just an unexpected opportunity to watch the clouds for a while.

Having to plan one's day by the clock at all is a bothersome necessity for the idler. Lin Yutang had it right when he said that: "A man who has to be punctually at a certain place at five o'clock has the whole afternoon from one to five ruined for him already." But at least Slow Watches are a step in the right direction.

An even more ambitious project of go-slow reinvention is underway at Monohm, a Californian start-up whose name is a portmanteau of the Japanese word "mono" (meaning "object"), and the unit of electrical resistance "ohm". They're developing a strikingly designed "anti-smartphone" called the Runcible – apart from the lingering doubt that it actually exists – a nonsense word, coined by Edward Lear for his 1871 poem *The Owl and the Pussycat*.

Modelled on a fob watch, the Runcible is shaped like a perfect circle. The cover can be made out of swamp ash or maple burl wood, or – if you want your Runcible to look like a high-tech pebble – mottled grey plastic. It slopes gently away from the camera lens in the centre (which will, of course, take circular photos), making the phone feel beautifully tactile. More eccentric users can clip their Runcible onto a chain and wear it in their waistcoat pocket.

As well as looking like your grandpa's fob watch, the Runcible will be just as durable. Monohm describe it as an "heirloom device": it's easy to replace or upgrade individual parts (like the camera

"It's all about wearable technology, these days."

or the hard-drive) without having to ditch the whole thing. When Monohm finally launch the Runcible for the mass market, expect it to come with a hefty price tag, to compensate them for forsaking built-in obsolescence.

Perhaps many years from now, undergraduate philosophy students won't be reading about Plutarch's *Ship of Theseus* or John Locke's *Sock*, but will instead hotly contest the problem of Grandad's Runcible, every part of which is a replacement.

If that is to come to pass, then the youth of today will have to ditch their affection for apps like Instagram and Snapchat, neither of which will be available on the Runcible. In fact, even the way the phone handles calls and SMS will be heavily pared-down. The Runcible won't shake around like billy-o when somebody rings you. Missed calls and texts will be displayed as gently expanding bubbles on the home screen, rather than as numerals next to drawings of a phone and an envelope. (Why does the phone drawing always look like a home phone from the 1970s, and never like a boring white rectangle with a half-eaten apple on the back?)

The most charming aspect of the Runcible is its anti-smartphone answer to the conventional street map. Instead of giving you an aerial view of where you need to get to, the Runcible's navigation app will transform it into a compass. The arrow will swing not to face due North, but rather to face towards wherever you want to go to. For committed idlers, the app will even (if Monohm goes through with this idea) divert you to places of interest nearby along your route, turning every city-walk into an adventure.

Something about the Runcible and the Slow Watch reminds me of Dada contraptions: things like bicycles that can't be ridden, and cameras that flash but don't have lenses. Like the Dada artists, users of Runcibles and Slow Watches care less about functionality than they care about having a reminder of how life is best lived.

This is all to the good, because there's a lot for the idler to admire in the philosophy of Dada. The Dada artists rejected logic in favour of intuition and impulse. They had a healthy appreciation of the value of nonsense, and a strong capacity for noticing the absurd in modern life. That old fooler Edward Lear would have enthusiastically approved. 🌀

For more details visit
slow-watches.com and mono.hm

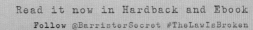

Poetry

How early is too early?

By **Murray Lachlan Young**

We got here too early for teleportation
We got here too early for journeys to Mars
We got here too early for AI domination
But we might get a trip in a driverless car

Yes a trip in a driverless car

As we scream through the universe strapped to the sun
Judging time by the minute and hour
Clinging to things that the tooth fairy brings
Going seventy thousand miles an hour

No clue of the reason of why we are here
Or which mother is really in charge
Unable to see how our brains are so small
Or indeed how disturbingly large

And so we create both the early and late
And the Gods that are right and are wrong
And the good and the bad and the sane and the mad
And we join in and all sing along along

Wearing clothes we suppose speak of up-to-date views
And the "what" and the "why" and the "how"
When the whole thing is nothing but star studded chaos
And *could* end in just a few seconds from now

Yes it in just a few seconds from now.

Because we got here too early for teleportation
We got here too early for journeys to Mars
We got here too late to own our own data
But we might get a trip in a driverless car

Yes a trip in a driverless car

MEDITATION PART ONE *with* Sister Jayanti, Director of European Countries at the Brahma Kumaris Spiritual University, leads our new meditation course. Jayanti has over 40 years of experience in Raja Yoga meditation and recently led the meditation sessions at Davos.

AN INTRODUCTION TO PSYCHOTHERAPY
with Dr Mark Vernon
Therapist Dr Vernon with a clear and concise six-part history and practice of psychotherapy, from Freud and Jung to Melanie Klein and modern thinkers.

HOW TO MAKE SOURDOUGH BREAD
with Bridget Hugo
The founder of Franco Manca pizza chain and Bread Bread bakery presents the ultimate guide to slow baking. Across 21 episodes in two-and-a-half hours of video, you will learn how to make delicious bread using just flour, water and salt.

HOW TO ESCAPE
with Robert Wringham
If you want to break free, this practical course will show you how.

A HISTORY OF WINE
with MW Anne McHale
The story of the grape from ancient times to the present day.

THE HAPPY KITCHEN
with Rachel Kelly
Learn how to make mood-enhancing recipes.

THE GUIDE TO IDLE BEEKEEPING
with Bill Anderson
Entertaining course on how to keep bees the easy and natural way.

THE IDLER GUIDE TO NEGOTIATION
with Hilary Gallo
A fascinating insight into the philosophy underpinning successful negotiation with former corporate lawyer Hilary.

HOW TO BUILD YOUR OWN UTOPIA

with David Bramwell

Join author David Bramwell for an inspiring journey to utopias around the world, and come back with ideas to improve your life right now.

HOW TO WRITE A SONG

with Chris Difford

The legendary lyricist from Squeeze, author of "Up the Junction" and "Cool for Cats", leads an interactive course in penning your own song.

A HISTORY OF LONDON

with Dr Matthew Green

The historian and Penguin author has consigned his considerable knowledge of London history to video form.

HOW TO WRITE A POEM

with Clare Pollard

Release your inner poet on this wonderful course.

CLASSICAL CIVILISATION

with Harry Mount

An efficient primer on the key happenings, movements and ideas in Greek and Roman civilisation.

A HISTORY OF CHRISTIANITY

with Dr Mark Vernon

Dr Vernon is back with this fantastic primer on the two thousand year evolution of Christianity.

BUSINESS FOR BOHEMIANS

An Introduction to Business for Creative People
with Tom Hodgkinson

Idler editor Tom has distilled the advice given in his book into ten handy classes for creative entrepreneurs.

LEARN LATIN

with Harry Mount

This three-part course takes you from beginner to undergraduate level and will really get your brain cells working. Suitable for all ages and great as a supplement to your child's school lessons.

ALSO AVAILABLE:

LEARN HARMONICA *with* Ed Hopwood

A HISTORY OF BRITISH BUILDINGS *with* Harry Mount

A GUIDE TO MODERN MANNERS *with* Mary Killen

THE IDLER GUIDE TO GROWING VEGETABLES AND HERBS
with Alys Fowler

ELOCUTION *with* Sir Timothy Ackroyd

HOW TO DRESS – A GUIDE FOR THE MODERN GENTLEMAN
with Gustav Temple

HOW TO BE IDLE *with* Tom Hodgkinson

AN INTRODUCTION TO MODERN PHILOSOPHY
with Dr Mark Vernon

EMINENT VICTORIANS *with* John Mitchinson

UKULELE FOR BEGINNERS *with* Danny Wootton

AN INTRODUCTION TO ANCIENT PHILOSOPHY
with Dr Mark Vernon

AN INTRODUCTION TO CLASSICAL MUSIC *with* Sandy Burnett

THE IDLER HISTORY OF COOKING IN SIX CHAPTERS
with Rowley Leigh

PUBLIC SPEAKING *with* David Butter

HOW TO SING *with* Diana de Cabarrus

BEYOND MINDFULNESS *with* Tim Lott

PUNCTUATION *with* Harry Mount

available at

IDLER.CO.UK/SHOP/ONLINE-COURSES

LIBERTAS PER CULTUM

Men are all alike.
IN WHAT WAY?

Men are all alike.
IN WHAT WAY?
They're always bugging
us about something
or other.

Interview

Adam Curtis

How do we get towards a new politics?
How do we stay human in an age of machine learning?
Tom Hodgkinson *asks the journalist and documentary-maker who has been watching the watchers for the past four decades*

FROM *The Century of the Self* to *Hypernormalisation*, the journalist Adam Curtis has consistently exposed stories and truths that lay hidden to others. On his BBC blogs he tells brilliantly researched features on, for example, the history of think tanks and their relationship with battery farming and Google. Always entertaining and always a provocative, original voice, he refuses to spout liberal platitudes and makes up his own mind. This bold voice has found him millions of fans across the world, and he is finding a new audience among the teens and twentysomethings.

We recorded two interviews and what follows is edited highlights from our discussions. We start by discussing the so-called power of the tech titans. Adam argues that a simple way to take away their power would be to stop believing in their magic.

ADAM CURTIS: When we say: "Facebook is a dark, manipulative force", it makes the people in charge seem extremely powerful. The truth is that people within the advertising and marketing industry are extremely suspicious about whether online advertising has any effect at all. The Internet has been captured by four giant corporations who don't produce anything, contribute nothing to the wealth of the country, and hoard their billions of dollars in order to pounce on anything that appears to be a competitor and buy it out immediately. They will get you and I to do the work for them – which is putting the data in – then they send out what they con other people into believing are targeted ads. But actually, the problem with their advertising is that it is – like all geek stuff – literal. It has no imagination to it whatsoever. It sees that you bought a ticket to Budapest, so you're going to get more tickets to Budapest. It's a scam.

"SOCIAL MEDIA IS A SCAM"

In a way, the whole Facebook/Cambridge Analytica thing played into their hands because it made it even more mystifying. I've always thought John Le Carré did spies a great service because he made it seem as if there were endless depths of mystery and darkness when in fact, if you've ever researched

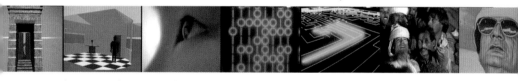

the spies, they are a) boring and b) useless. I mean really, really useless. I researched MI5 once and they hardly ever manage to capture any traitors ... it's usually someone else who points them in the right direction. And in a way I think that's true of this. The tech companies are powerful in the sense that they've got hold of the Internet, which people like me think could be a really powerful thing for changing the world and disseminating new ideas, and they've got it in this rigid headlock. To do that, they've conned everyone into thinking that their advertising is worth it. And in the process, they're destroying journalism.

TOM HODGKINSON: Cambridge Analytica and Facebook are surely clever and manipulative though?

AC I'm sure some really bad stuff went on. There's no question about that. But where's the evidence that it actually swayed elections? What we lost in the hysteria about it all, is the sense of: why did people really vote for Brexit and Trump? I maintain that all the evidence points to the fact that there is real anger and a sense of isolation in Britain and America. The results reflected that. For 20 years, they've been offered no choice between the political parties. They've been given this enormous button that says "Fuck off" and they've pressed it. That's a rational thing to do.

"WHAT DO THEY ACTUALLY KNOW ABOUT YOU? YOUR SHOPPING?"

The problem with the professional classes is that they don't know how to deal with that. Instead they turn to these other reasons, which of course are there. But it's like they're looking at a little part of something much, much bigger, which involves having to make political choices about what might have gone wrong in your society. Everyone goes: "Oh that's magical!" about the Internet, but so what? That's actually just so banal. People go: "Oh it's terrible, they're manipulating us!" or: "They know so much about me!" Well, what do they know about you? Your shopping? That's it? What they *don't* know, actually, are all the things that *you've* forgotten which are your real intelligence, and that world that you live in in your head, day by day – which is rich and extraordinary.

TH That's a lovely thought. So we should really be saying they're stupid and they're boring?

AC Yes, and all they really know about you is your shopping.

"WE ARE EXTRAORDINARY AND WE CAN DO EXTRAORDINARY THINGS"

TH There are good things about the Internet.

AC The Internet is all sorts of things. The real problem is that we've grown up in a period of high individualism and, in a period of high individualism, the one thing you don't notice is power. You're supposed to be an empowered individual yourself. What's disappeared out of the language is power. We just don't see it. We just blindly go through the world, not seeing that there are powerful forces.

TH We tweet instead.

AC We're in this very funny paradoxical moment in history, which is full of moments of dynamic hysteria, yet everything always remains the same. We get this wave of hysteria – angry people click more! – and those clicks feed the systems and nothing changes. It's a rational machine model. The idea of Artificial Intelligence is a very limited, machine-like idea. What we're ignoring is all those other aspects of human beings, which we don't really acknowledge because they're so inbuilt in us and have been for millions of years.

TH Like the romantic side of life?

AC It's partly the romantic side but it's also our ability to move through a cluttered environment, like a street – while dreaming of extraordinary images and visions of things that have never happened, but just come from the depths of no one knows what. I mean the thing is our scientists have no real idea what consciousness is – so I think it's a bit difficult to build some form of real intelligence when you don't even know how your own one really works. So the tech AI people are in the midst of a massive PR drive to persuade us that really we are no more than simple machines – which means we will agree humbly to be fitted into their stupid machine decision trees. We think

intelligence is about playing Go. But practically no one plays Go. Or chess. Real intelligence is being able to walk through an incredibly crowded street on a busy evening, nimbly, when you don't even think about it, while at the same time recalling memories and replaying things in your brain. What I'm saying is that human beings have been reduced to a very simplified version of themselves, which they've accepted, in order to fit into this machine model, both of society and the Internet. But we are extraordinary and we can do extraordinary things. We are so much more than what they are forcing us to accept.

TH So where should we be looking for the positive ideas? In *Hypernormalisation* you make the point that people have retreated, the politicians are just managers, there's no vision of the future. Or there is, but it's a bit negative.

AC Or apocalyptic.

TH Can you see anyone around the world, writers, politicians, anybody who's got something positive to say?

AC Well, I'm sure there is someone somewhere because things do change. I'm a journalist and journalists are very good at analysing what is happening now and trying to report it. I suspect you have to look at the two things that have been marginalised in this static world. One is science, and one is religion. Science has gone from something that in its glory days was going to change the world to becoming an adjunct of the dark doomsayers which just tells you if you eat this you will die. It's become co-opted by the managerial system, it's about how many pieces of fruit you should eat each day and it's a debate between seven and 15 I think [*laughs*]. And, it's got stuck because there are all these things that it can't explain. For example, it tells you that there is stuff called dark matter but they know it's there because they can't see it which is remarkably like the weapons of mass destruction in Iraq. It means it's lost its purchase on our imagination of awesomeness. The other thing is religion. Religion is waiting in the wings because in an age of individualism, the one thing that you cannot deal with is the idea of your own mortality. You cannot conceive of what lies beyond you because the world *is* you. I think part of the apocalyptic mood of our time, part of it, not all of it, is coming from the baby boomer generation beginning to face the

"THE REAL POLITICS OF THE FUTURE WILL HAVE TO ALLOW YOU TO FEEL THAT YOU ARE BOTH AN INDIVIDUAL AND IN CONTROL OF YOUR OWN DESTINY"

inevitable fact of their mortality and they're a bit like Ayn Rand. When she was asked: "Don't you fear death?" she said: "No, of course not, because *I* won't die, the world will die." What she means is that, if you are an arch individual like she was, the world is in your head and that's it. And that is a very lonely place to be. What religion is really doing is offering consolation in the fear of death: there's something beyond you.

TH Particularly before the Reformation, the whole point of the church was that if you live your life well and religiously you'll be saved and go to heaven.

AC But we captured that idea in this country with socialism which co-opted those religious ideas and said we can work together to create something that will be great in the future, not necessarily for you, but for other people. Look, the real politics of the future is going to have to square the circle. It's going to have to allow you to still feel that you are an individual and in control of your own destiny.

TH Isn't that anarchism?

AC No it isn't anarchism. To be honest, anarchism has been captured by the notion of individualism just like everything else has, just like Thatcher was. What I'm talking about is something I wouldn't give an *old* term to ....

TH What could it be called?

AC Its roots are going to lie in two places: one is the fusion of keeping the idea of individualism yet giving you a sense of being part of something, but you are not a slave to it, and the other is that you are going to re-energise the idea of science and fuse it to the idea that there is a purpose to your life. And the Internet is the thing that could do it, except the bastards have got hold of it and done the opposite and have isolated us even more. We are being made to do this work for free for them and they feed us stuff and we remain in our little bubbles. Well that's wrong. I mean in a way, I would argue for the

nationalisation of the Internet.

TH To become a public utility?

AC Yes, in which people can configure it in a way in which you don't have to make money out of it. It's there, it works.

TH Like Royal Mail. The Royal Internet!

AC No, I'm not going to join your folky world [*laughs*] – that's the bit I divide from you on. What I'm saying is that this is a very limited view of society, it's a management view of society. Meanwhile Trump is a distraction. He has really provided us a pantomime villain. He wakes up in the morning, gets his smartphone, tweets something really outrageous. Within nanoseconds, the managerial liberals are looking at their smartphones going: "This is outrageous, typical capitalist, how can he say this?" At which point, they're locked into a feedback loop of anger, fury and outrage. Meanwhile, outside the theatre, outside the pantomime, people like Mike Pence, and all the large techno financial, managerial complex are quietly getting on with what they really want to do, which is things like privatising armies. Really, they are. The managerial liberals are locked in the theatre with Trump. And that is where all our journalism has gone.

"WHAT YOU HAVE TO DO IS GO AND READ BOOKS. IN BOOKS YOU WILL FIND EXTRAORDINARY STORIES"

TH Are there any online news sources that you would guide people to, or books?
AC I know everyone says there's massive amount of information on the Internet but actually, if you analyse it, there is very little. It tends to be the same thing repeated over and over again. This is something to do with Google rankings; it's also something to do with the speed with which journalism must be done. So what you have to do is go and read books. Read really boring, old books. Among the academic rubbish, and the very badly written academic phraseology, there are really good stories.

That thing about Trump and the Japanese gambler in *Hypernormalisation*

– that was in a very boring book on gambling. In books you will find extraordinary stories. I'm very interested in the way, for example, money was set free from the 1970s onwards, there was no longer the benchmark of using the dollar to have fixed exchange rates. So money just became this free-floating thing that began to eat away at all politics. Until 1980, credit card companies were only allowed to charge a certain level of interest. What happened was the finance companies lobbied, and got it removed in 1980. It was only going to be temporary but actually it has stayed there. I went onto the Internet and I couldn't find anything about it, so then, using Nexis, which most people don't have access to, I tracked down some funny old books in the British Library and have now discovered that it was pushed forward by one congressman from Rhode Island who was bribed by the finance companies. They gave him five "International House of Pancake" [IHOP] outlets as a bribe. [IHOP is a chain of breakfast-themed diners in the US].
TH What, as a reward?

AC Yes it was their bribe, this was their way of disguising it. They actually bought him five IHOPs and gave them to him.

TH The IHOP conspiracy!

AC So the reason payday loans companies are allowed to charge you 6,000% interest is because of the five IHOPs. I found that in a really dusty old book in the British Library.

TH So can you do what you want at the BBC?

AC No. I'm employed at the BBC, I produce for the BBC, I put forward ideas to them, they say yes or no. The freedom I get is really because I don't have to go out and film stuff. I can chop and change and chop and change and I always go find out the stuff. It's much more like writing.

TH Also it's fairly low cost for the BBC.

AC I charge them absolutely nothing in terms of the programme budget. *Hypernormalisation* cost £32,000, which is nothing.

TH Are you a PAYE employee?

AC Yes, I'm a member of the staff. And I take it very seriously. I think they quite like me because I'm very affectionate to the BBC. I praise them. It's a chaotic

"WHEN YOU SAY AWFUL, TERRIBLE THINGS ON FACEBOOK, YOU'RE ACTUALLY FEEDING FACEBOOK"

and sometimes out-of-control organisation, which of course I love, because I can swim between the cracks. They give me immense freedom. There is a joke about me at the BBC – an exec said to me: "You know what we call you? A fig leaf." When [the BBC] is accused of dumbing down they can point at me and say: "Look at him, he does pretentious shit" [*laughs*].

TH You have many young fans though. My daughter, who is 16, is a fan of yours. She said, "Really, you're going to see Adam Curtis?!"

AC I actually have great faith in the ones below the millennials. They seem to be really political. *Hypernormalisation* has somehow cut through, and I don't think it was because of the music. They showed it in a cinema in LA for five nights last year. Every night there were queues around the block and many of them were 16–18 year olds.

TH They seem to be waking up to the fact that Twitter and Facebook use the doctrine of "self-expression" to sell ads and make billions.

AC I got into trouble because I gave an interview in an art magazine in America where I said I am deeply suspicious about the idea of radical art being able to change the system because the system is based on the idea of self-expression. That's central to modern consumer capitalism. The idea that if you buy those trainers, you're expressing yourself. I mean that however radical your actual content in your artwork is, the underlying way you are doing it – through self-expression – is in a sense feeding the very system you are trying to undermine. You're actually bloating it. When you say awful, terrible things on Facebook, you're actually feeding Facebook.

To go back to the question of what the new politics might be, one of things people will have to do is give up the idea they're expressing themselves. I think that's going to be one of the most difficult things in our age. I've always thought one of the great underlying dynamics of our time is the self-consciousness of every individual, the sense that they feel they're being watched. You would actually have to give that up and say I'm working for

this goal or for other people, but what it needs to go with that is a really good idea. It needs to be a really imaginative idea. You have to actually make an effort.

To go back to your question about where new ideas come from. They will come from odd corners. I got fascinated quite a long time ago by the Kurds. I found out that the guy in charge of the PKK [Kurdish Workers' Party], a man called [Abdullah] Öcalan, had become obsessed in his prison cell with the writings of an American anarchist called Murray Bookchin, and that the towns in Northern Syria are actually anarchist experiments. And no one knows about it.

TH Why is that not reported? Someone told me to go out there and hang out with them.

AC I wouldn't at the moment. The Turks would bomb you and the tanks are just outside. *Vice* has been there.

TH I found *Vice* disappointing. There was a millisecond where I thought that *Vice* was an interesting magazine, but it's just sensationalist titillation.

AC No, I think you should be nicer to *Vice*. *Vice* really did transform journalism.

TH I find it prurient: "Hey we found a guy with his head chopped off", quite Beavis and Buttheady.

AC No. That's really unfair. They got in to Syria, were brave, and they showed us what it was like way before my organisation did. That was an amazing piece of journalism.

TH You talk about Occupy in your film. I remember at the time being quite excited by it.

"I DISLIKED GEORGE ORWELL'S TONE. IT WAS PATRONISING AND SNOTTY"

AC I thought it was going to be fantastic. But it wasn't. They had a great slogan, they came at the right moment, and they had lots of people who would not normally think of themselves as radical supporting them. I went down there and I saw it all, and I thought it was absolutely great. Then they blew it. It wasn't because they stopped. I'll tell you why they blew it, because they

bought in to this naïve idea of democracy. They confused process with ideas. It's as simple as that. They thought if you have a managerial process, where you and I and ten other people sit around, that out of that there will come an idea. It doesn't. That's a process.

TH What are your views on George Orwell and Aldous Huxley?

AC I don't know anything about them.

TH Weren't they saying similar things to what you're saying?

AC I have no idea. I've never read them. I tried reading some of George Orwell's essays, and I disliked his tone. It was patronising and snotty. And it's not funny.

TH He's not really funny, no. Aldous Huxley is a bit funny; *Brave New World* is hilarious.

AC I've never read it.

TH I thought these would have been canonical texts for you.

AC No. You've got to remember I'm a hack. I'm a journalist. I tried academia, I did it for about six months and I loathed it.

TH But hacks read Huxley and Orwell as well.

AC Do they? Not many I know.

TH Absolutely. I do!

AC You're not a hack, you're a magazine publisher [*laughs*]. One of my first jobs at *That's Life* was to go undercover at a puppy farm.

TH You were on *That's Life!*

AC That's where my career started.

"MY TRAINING IS TELEVISION TABLOID. SO I WOULD NEVER USE A WORD LIKE 'NEO-LIBERALISM'"

TH Are you Oxbridgey?

AC I went to Oxford. I did science. They offered me to do a PhD at Nuffield College, and I couldn't bear it. It's such a lonely life to be a PhD student and I'm very social. You have to go and find something that no one else has done,

at which point you're on your own [*laughs*]. So I gave it up. I stumbled into a job at the BBC working on *That's Life*. I decided to go into trash television.

TH When was that?

AC In the 1980s. I did undercover reporting, and then I did short films – talking animals and things like that. They key thing I took from trash journalism is how to make jokes. And the one real rule is: people who think they are funny are not funny, and people who think are they really serious can be really funny. That's the only rule you learn in trash journalism. I took that and I bolted it together with posh, high-end bollocks. My training is television tabloid. So I would never use a word like "neo-liberalism". Or "existentialism". I really hate the way certain kinds of journalists use phrases that they know will only be understood by those who already agree with them. You can say anything clearly and if you want to, you can put a cut-away of a dog in and you'll get a laugh. Then I decided that television journalism, especially documentaries, not observational documentaries, the ones that told you about the world, were so boring, so humourless, and have such shit music.

STRANGE ALLIANCE

There is one thing that I think is rather odd in all the confusion swirling around Trump and the Russians. It's the strange alliance that has been formed between the liberal journalists and the intelligence agencies. In particular, I mean the *New York Times* and *Washington Post* journalists – it's very clear that those journalists really want to get Trump, which means somehow impeaching him. And the CIA and the FBI are terrified that Trump will either reform them or diminish their role, so they want to get him too. And the spooks have started leaking all kinds of stuff – including secretly recorded conversations from people around Trump – to the journalists.

"I know all kinds of dirty stuff has happened forever in politics. But this is a bit odd – and risky for the liberals. First, they have hated the intelligence agencies for a long time – remember, these were the people who brought you WMD, and then tortured hundreds of often completely innocent people in secret jails around the world. So they are not really the best friends you could choose.

"Secondly, I know that the journalists and the spies really believe that they are doing this for the greater good of America – that it's really important to remove this weird, out-of-control sociopath. But then look at it from the point of view of a serious Trump supporter. They see something else: two very powerful, but unelected groups working together to undermine the democratically elected president. It's what was called Deep State in Turkey in the mid-1980s: intelligence agencies working with other unelected groups to bring down a democratically-elected government.

"So, from the point of view of a Trump supporter, when Trump tweets about Deep State, he really might have a point. To the liberals and spies that is stupid, because they know in their hearts that what they are doing is in the best interests of the state. But careful – that could really blow back on them. And spies have a habit of dropping their new best friends when the political reality changes.

ADAM CURTIS

"THINK TANKS VERY PRECISELY
STOP THINKING"

I have a theory that one of the great destructive forces in our modern age politics are think tanks. They have erected a wall around Westminster, and they've persuaded politicians that they are just managers of micro-policies. Think tanks very precisely stop thinking. They just want to manage a system as it is, whether they're left wing or right wing. They keep this going by feeding stuff into politics, people from think tanks go in to MPs. And they also do one other thing, they give you – for free – interviewees for 24-hour news. So 24-hour news and think tanks work together to freeze politics behind this protective wall.

TH And isn't the fundamental flaw with them is that they are always going to reflect the views of people who fund them?

AC Yes, it becomes a self-referencing system. And many of the think-tankers then become journalists as well. They all talk like think-tankers and what they do is managerial speak. I don't mean in a technical sense, their mindset is: you are here to manage things, and you micro-manage things to make it all a bit better. And I go back to my question, what is it all for? They have no idea.◉

Interview

Trip advisor

We meet **Michael Pollan**, *author of an excellent new book about psychedelics, which argues that guided trips could heal both individual and social wounds. As they dissolve the ego, they could usefully be administered to President Trump*

BOOKS about drugs can be deadly dull. They tend to be either tediously technical or horribly shamanic and humourless. Michael Pollan's new book, the brilliantly titled *How to Change Your Mind*, is neither. It is a very readable and funny account of a 60 year-old man's experiments with magic mushrooms, LSD and the fabled venom of the toad, and is a worthy successor to Aldous Huxley's *Doors of Perception*.

Mr Pollan's book is symptomatic of a wider renaissance in psychedelic studies, and explores – wittily and non-hysterically – what it is like to take a trip. He takes aim at Timothy Leary who derailed the serious research that was going on around psychedelics in the 1960s, and argues for a measured, sane, evidence-based approach to the use of mushrooms and LSD as a therapeutic aid. I was particularly struck by the way the book explores the way taking mushrooms can allay fears of death, because of the way they quieten the chattering ego. When we chatted, we naturally came to the conclusion that Donald Trump should try some.

TOM HODGKINSON How did you come to write this book?
MICHAEL POLLAN You should know that I started out terrified of psychedelics. I am a child of the moral panic against them. I was 14 during Woodstock and 12 in the Summer of Love. I remember terrible stories of people ending up in emergency rooms, going blind, jumping out of windows, and even cutting their wrists on acid trips.

So that is where I start from. But I was intensely curious to conduct this expedition into a foreign and somewhat scary world. I am thought of as a

Finding an azzie in Pacific Northwest

food journalist: actually my work is all about the human relationship with natural world.

I learned that the desire to use fungi and psychedelics is universal: there is only one culture in the world without psychoactive plants, and that is the Inuits, because nothing psychoactive grows where they live.

"THE WORLD WE SEE IS THE NOT THE ONLY WORLD OR EVEN THE MOST FAITHFUL TRANSCRIPTION OF REALITY"

I talked to a physicist who said that it was an LSD trip at 15 that opened him to the bizarre idea that particles don't exist until they are perceived, implausible as that may seem. The world we see is the not the only world or even the most faithful transcription of reality, and that set him on the path of examining these other realities.

TH Did you come across Terence McKenna [ethnobotanist, profiled in *Idler* issue 1, died April 2000]?

MP Yes and his hypothesis is that magic mushrooms wrought changes in our

Shrine in underground trip room

hominid ancestors and shaped our biological evolution. Enough mushrooms put selective pressure on the species, and language appeared, which is a variety of synaesthesia. Animals can hear colours and see sounds, while language is a special case where you connect meaningless sounds to concepts.

"PSILOCYBIN CAN HELP MAKE YOUR OWN PERSONAL EXTINCTION SEEM LESS TRAGIC"

TH You say that psilocybin, the active ingredient in magic mushrooms, has been used in medical contexts?

MP There were two studies in 2016, at NYU and John Hopkins, giving psilocybin to patients who had had terminal cancer diagnoses and were dealing with existential distress, anxiety, fear and depression. The results were quite striking – 80% of them had reductions in their anxiety and depression that lasted at least six months.

Many of them came back with a conviction that consciousness could survive death. Some of them – not all – experienced the death of the ego and that has big implications. It may have served as a death rehearsal. It makes you realise what makes death so terrifying: it is that this separate entity is

67

The treatment room at NYU

going to be extinguished. But if you define your first person as embracing community and nature and something beyond the I, then your personal extinction can seem less tragic.

TH Tell us about your own experiences.

MP I found some underground guides who do something much like the medical trials. I tried LSD, psilocybin, ayahuasca and DMT – in that I smoked the venom of a poisonous toad. This is sometimes referred to as the "Everest of psychedelics".

I took four grams of mushrooms, which is the approximate amount used with trials. With psilocybin you experience the dissolution of ego. Your instincts tell you to fight, but the guide tells you give in. And once you surrender you realise something quite extraordinary, which is that you are not identical to your ego. You become almost dispassionate, unperturbed, undefensive – as there is nothing to be defended any more, the wall has been lowered. You suddenly feel as if consciousness, subjectivity, is evenly spread over the world.

A guided psychedelic trip is very different from taking a trip while wandering around. You have eyeshades on and music on headphones. The idea is to make this a natural trip, and it succeeds. I also realised what a

A specimen of psilocybin azurescens growing in woodchips

remarkably powerful piece of technology an eyeshade is. You tend to revisit things in your life. You experience an introspective-psychic movie, heavily determined by the music that is playing. You are open to suggestion. Some music will put you in a rainforest; some music will put you in the desert; other in a weird computer world.

It was a very interesting and useful experience. I saw my father from a different perspective; I saw him as a son and experienced a flood of compassion for him.

Aldous Huxley says consciousness is a "reducing valve", which keeps things out of our awareness, as the mind is not interested in taking in any more auditory and visual info than it needs to survive. Our consciousness is a filter – there is more to this world than meets the eye. There is that great line: "The world is full of magic things patiently waiting for our senses to grow sharper" [often attributed to Yeats or Bertrand Russell but in fact coined by obscure author Eden Phillpotts].

Your senses get a lot more acute. And the ego is keeping internal material from our awareness too, and that includes trauma. Without that patrolman or security guard, patrolling the walls between and you and your past, all sorts of things are likely to enter your conscious awareness.

Michael has the contents of his mind measured
and manipulated at Jud Brewer's lab

You are advised that if you see anything monstrous, you should move towards it. I saw a mountain lion: don't turn tail and run – hold your ground, and look very large.

An overactive ego can mire you in rumination, and you can become addicted to certain kinds of behaviour; the ego can reinforce your destructive nature.

TH These egotists in Silicon Valley are very successful, however. Take for example the billionaire investor Peter Thiel.

MP Yes and this is not to demonise the ego. The ego is dynamic, and accomplishes a lot. It got this book written.

Thiel has actually invested in psychedelic research, and is very engaged is what is called the "life-hacking" community.

In Berkeley, where I live, there are overlaps between hippies and techno-utopians. Silicon Valley has become very interested in psychedelics. The early computer engineers discovered LSD; many found it very useful for their work. Steve Jobs has talked about how important LSD trips were to his development.

"THE RISE OF TRIBALISM CAN ACTUALLY BE ADDRESSED BY PSYCHEDELIC EXPERIENCES"

The life hacking community is trying to extend life, download consciousness on to computers and live forever.

Some of the tech guys are using LSD that way, as a performance drug, taking tiny doses to give them a mental edge. Many are exploring large doses to nurture their spiritual side.

TH Now what is happening in your country with Trump?

MP Well, he's taking up a lot of headspace. In a way he's been a boon to journalism. Newspaper and magazines sales are up and people can't get enough of him.

I never would have predicted that two full years into his presidency that we would still be interested. He has altered the story line so many times and we have not got bored.

It's possible that the rise of tribalism can actually be addressed by psychedelic experiences, because these sorts of trips diminish our sense of separateness, and nurture a sense of connection and universality. So it seems to me to be a useful tool, and it's popping up right now, at a time it could prove beneficial to people.

TH Give the president acid! Now, how would *Idler* readers get involved in this?

MP There are extensive trials going on in Europe, particularly in the use of psilocybin, for treatment-resistant depression. In the UK these are taking place at Imperial College. Also the practice of holotropic breath work can produce a trance which is totally legal, and you can find people who will administer that. This is not for everyone, but you can find the underground guys out there. The real point is that we are learning important things about the consciousness, and what psychedelics can teach us about the mind. 🐌

How to Change Your Mind: The New Science of Psychedelics (*Allen Lane*) is out now.

Picture story

Psycho weeds

Idler *art director* **Alice Smith** *introduces her illustrations of mind-bending plants*

AROUND two years ago I began working on a project called "Worts", an illustrative study of the dangers and medicinal qualities of weeds. "Worts" is an old word for medicinal weed plants. The pictures reproduced here, "Psycho weeds", are an offshoot of that project.

"Worts" started as an exercise in memory. I was looking at the plants that spring up in the cracks of pavements, buildings' crevices and roadside carpets. I recognised them but forgot their names and uses, so I started to read up about them, making notes, collaging and drawing botanical and medical elements, and combining them to communicate the biology, folk-lore and scientific knowledge of each plant's story into one single illustration. This would help remind me of how and for what reason I might use each plant. It's now growing into a large book project.

I created "Psycho Weeds" because psychoactive plants are often dangerous and they don't sit comfortably within "Worts". I would never use these plants medicinally. Most are toxic to eat and need processing to extract the psycho-active chemical.

It's a fascinating and complex subject … but I won't be making home brews and potions from these plants. 🐌

More of these illustrations will be available as art prints at Alice's stall at the Idler festival in July. See idler.co.uk and alice-smith.co.uk for details.

Belladonna
Atropa belladonna

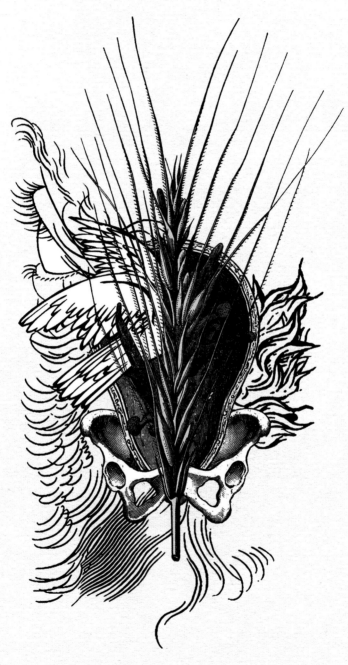

Ergot
Claviceps purpurea

Opium
Papaver somniferum

Wild Lettuce
Lactuca virosa

Valerian
Valerianaceae officinalis

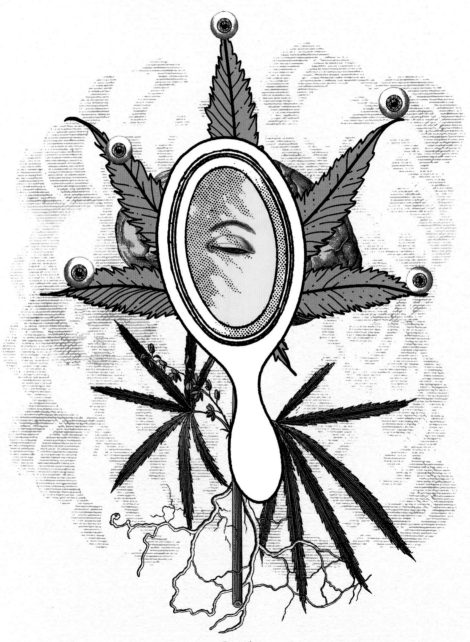

Cannabis
Cannabis sativa

Angel's Trumpets
Datura stramonium

Cricket

The lethargic pageant

In which **Joe Mellen** *opens his memory hole back to days spent in the blissful grip of white flannelled men upon the village green*

LOAD my senses: fill my brain with the sweet memories of childhood days under chestnut trees. White-flannelled fielders poised on the village green as the bowler trundles up to the wicket. Picnicking families on tartan rugs – pass the cucumber-and-Marmite sandwiches. A round of applause for a meaty drive across the slightly bumpy grass to the whitewashed boundary lines marked out by the hand-pushed dispenser (somewhat unromantically called an FW10 application line-marker) that got snagged on specially tough tufts as it was wheeled along by one of the club's old faithfuls.

A lethargic pageant played out across the land, the sumptuous sound of the stitch-seamed red leather sphere hitting the sweet spot in the middle of the willow blade as the master batsman bends his knees and follows through, elbow in line with the ball's intended destination, in a perfect off-drive through the covers – then the nostril-tickling scent of linseed oil being rubbed into the bat to keep it well-oiled for a juicy impact. That subtle scent of summer days – I remember sitting in the pavilion at prep school, soaking up the whole glorious atmosphere, two fingers caressing the oil to ooze into the grain until it had disappeared and the blade glowed with a healthy reward for the labour of love ... It's not the same today with the plastic covers on the bats.

My headmaster had played for Yorkshire, that paramount county that only its own sons could represent and, so the story went, he'd almost been picked for England. At any rate, he was a sadistic bastard, who loved nothing better than thrashing little boys' buttocks with a bamboo cane – he took a three-pace run across the library carpet to attack the taut buttocks beneath the pyjama trousers facing him, with the offender's face hidden beneath the overturned dressing gown, head-down on the sofa. His wrists were made of steel. Nowadays, he'd probably be in prison, but "spare the rod and spoil the child" was the mantra of those days.

Vintage virtual

While I was at that school, in the late 1940s, I played a Splodge Cricket County Championship. Now this is a relic of virtual sport from bygone days – boys don't have the time for that sort of thing now they've got computers. What was needed for this performance was a rather large, hand-drawn grid in which each square was marked with the possible results of a ball bowled: a dot for no run, then the numbers 1–6 for runs scored (allocated roughly in proportion to their likely occurrence), then dismissals, (B for bowled, LBW, CT for caught, RO for run out, etc) also spread sparingly across the grid.

A scorecard was filled with the names of the two teams in batting order and then, most important, the bowling analysis. This was another grid, with the bowler's name on the left beside one line of the grid. As each ball was bowled it was recorded in the box, so at the end of the over there were six marks in it, indicating dots, runs, wickets etc.

The way the virtual game progressed was by dropping a pin on to the large grid and then marking the result in the scorecard, so the bowler's box would record his over and, if runs were scored, they were placed in the horizontal row opposite the batsman's name. If a wicket was taken it was recorded appropriately – if it was caught, a pin was dropped on the opposition's team to determine which fielder caught it. As you can imagine, a single game would take an enormous amount of time to complete, hours and hours. To get through the entire county championship (albeit a knock-out format) was an extraordinarily laborious process, but I completed it. It was a satisfying pastime, combining my love for the game with my love of writing and neatness.

Net interest

One can't write about cricket without mentioning the nets. For the uninitiated, someone from a foreign field that is not forever England perhaps, the nets are arrangements of artificial pitches side by side, divided by nets, with a back net stretched across them all. It is a practice ground. The batsman takes his place at the back of the net in front of the three stumps (with bails on or not) and the bowler bowls to him from the other end.

The ball is stopped from disappearing by the nets, so that it is returned to the bowler for another go. At least in theory that's the idea, though a good number of nets end up with holes in vital places, so that frequently someone has to run and retrieve the lost ball. *Tant pis.* In this way the whole process is speeded up and the batsman can "get his eye in" before going out to bat in the real game.

To this day, you will see nets in public spaces. My son Rudy and I used to use nets on Clapham Common and also in the beautiful Brockwell Park in Brixton, but you will find them in parks and recreation grounds across the land.

Wicketing wonders

The roll call of the greats rings out, from those halcyon days before TV: Hobbs, Hammond, Hutton, WG – the bearded master. Herbert Sutcliffe, Patsy Hendren, Jim Laker and Tony Lock, Ramadhin and Valentine, the spin twins from the Windies, immortalised in the calypso of that name. Johnny Wardle, Tom Graveney, Bill Edrich and Denis Compton, the batting terrors of Middlesex in 1947, both scoring over 3,000 runs in the season. Larwood and Voce, Statham and Trueman, Alec Bedser, Derek Underwood's fast trundling spinners, Peter May, Colin Cowdrey…

I remember lying on the ground by the newly-constructed swimming pool at Eton in the glorious summer of 1956 and listening to the almost unbelievable progress of Jim Laker's off-breaks bamboozling the Aussies at Old Trafford. The team led by Lindsay Hassett included the mercurial Keith Miller (he was always called "mercurial"), Arthur Morris (Bradman had gone by now), Ray Lindwall, Neil Harvey, Richie Benaud and the rest of the squad that had been dubbed "The Invincibles". Nine for 35, Laker took in the first innings, which was incredible, considering that Tony Lock was bowling at the other end and he was also brilliant.

Then in the second innings he was at it again – could it happen? One by one they fell, the batsmen surrounded by a ring of close fielders like piranhas waiting to snap up the slightest snick … And glory be, he got the lot, ten for 53, 19 wickets in the match – it had never happened before in any form of cricket and it will probably never happen again.

Fast-forward to 1981 and the mighty Botham stepping into the crease in the second Ashes Test. Beefy, as he was known to one and all, had flunked his First Test as captain, England losing by four wickets and one down in the series. Mike Brearley took over as captain at the Second Test at Headingley, whereupon England were outplayed and made to follow on. Australia made 401 for 9 declared, England were skittled for 174.

In the second innings, we were 41 for four when Beefy came to the wicket. More wickets quickly fell, until at 135 for seven, Beefy said to his partner, Graham Dilley: "Right, let's have a bit of fun!" and proceeded to lay into the Aussie attack. Sixes followed fours, then more sixes. At close of stumps he was 145 not out – the Aussies didn't know what had hit them. In the morning he added another four, before the last man was out. By then England had a lead of 124. It was a formality for Australia to knock off the runs, but then the unbelievable happened. Bob Willis took eight for 43 and the Aussies were skittled for 111, their unlucky number. It was only the second time in history that a team made to follow on had won the game. Botham's innings had knocked the stuffing out of the goose.

Later Beefy was made a knight of the realm, Sir Ian Botham, potsmoker *extraordinaire*, the greatest all-rounder England's ever produced, but perhaps not the greatest of all. That accolade must be reserved for Sir Garfield Sobers, the West Indian genius. At 21 he made the highest ever score in a test match, 365 not out, and Gary was not only a brilliant batsman but also a devastating fast-medium bowler, with his slingy action. In 1968 he became the first cricketer to hit six sixes in an over, playing for Notts against Glamorgan – Malcolm Nash was the unfortunate bowler (though he admits that he has dined out on the story ever since). The fifth ball was caught on the boundary, but the fielder stepped over the boundary line with the ball in his hand, so it was given as a six. Quite rightly, Gary was knighted too, as earlier had Len Hutton been, England's first professional captain, and herein lies a tale.

Knights in white flannel

When I was a boy, in the 1940s and 1950s, cricketers were divided into Gentlemen and Players. I kid you not. Every year there was a match at Lords between those two teams. The Gentlemen were amateurs, the Players professional. Amateurs were not paid. In the scorecard they were accorded the honour of having the prefix Mr attached to their names. They played for the love of it. How they made ends meet I'm not sure – I think they were sponsored by rich cricket-lovers. Colin Cowdrey was sponsored by a friend of my father's, Dick Wilkins, a podgy cricket lover and wealthy denizen of the City, who paid for Cowdrey to go to Oxford. Captains of county teams and England in those days were always amateurs who'd usually played for Oxford or Cambridge before joining their county. Len Hutton broke the mould and he was knighted too! The distinction between amateurs and professionals was ended in 1962.

A few other cricketers have been knighted, as is only right for players of the prince of games: for England, Gubby Allen, Alec Bedser, Jack Hobbs, Baron Colin Cowdrey and David Sheppard, who became a bishop and then a life peer. For New Zealand, Richard Hadlee; obviously the great, the one and only Don Bradman for Australia, and a handful of the great West Indies sides of the 1970s and 1980s, the three Ws, Frank Worrell, Everton Weekes and Clyde Walcott, and Wes Hall and Curtly Ambrose of those hurricane bowlers and the master blaster, Viv Richards.

For India, Ranjitsinhji was a maharajah. Then there was the Nawab of Pataudi. I first came across him playing for my prep school, Ludgrove. We played Locker's Park, a rival school. In their team was this 11-year-old, Pataudi. He took eight wickets and caught the other two. Then he knocked off the runs required with consummate ease. He was a prodigy. He made his first-class debut for Sussex in 1957 at the age of 16 before going up to Oxford where he was the first Indian to captain the team. In 1961 he was involved in a car crash and lost the sight of one eye. This didn't deter him from playing the game he loved and he went on to captain India, scoring six test centuries with his cap pulled down over his sightless eye. God knows what a career he would have had with two good eyes!

It is noticeable that only one Aussie is included in this list, though they have been our oldest and greatest rivals – perhaps this is why, because over the years they have probably given us more heartache than any other country. Unconsciously we resent the pupils (not to say colonial subjects) teaching the masters how to play!

Batting on acid

My own cricketing life was not a story of unending success. I liked to do a bit of everything, bowling left-handed chinamen (out of the back of the hand) or medium-pacers and opening the batting. I just made the First 11 at prep school, though to be honest my highest score as opener was a paltry 14! At Eton I got strawberry mess, a cap, deep pink with white horizontal stripes, which could, if somewhat generously, be called the Third 11. I came into my own in house cricket. We were a wet-bob house, which meant that most boys rowed. I became captain of the house team towards the end of my career there, and scored quite a few runs in inter-house matches, even the odd 50. As I was captain, I could put myself on to bowl whenever I wanted, so I usually opened the bowling as well as the batting, and took quite a few wickets too.

Later in life I played village cricket, which I enjoyed a lot. It was about the right level for my skills, which were very far from first or even second-class. The rustic game on the village green was what could be referred to as "on the agricultural side". But it was played with great enthusiasm and the village teams would include players from every walk of life, old, young, farmers, landowners and tenants, blacksmiths, city gents, gamekeepers, a cross-section of English country life.

Tea was made by one or more of the wives consisting of sandwiches, home-made cakes and biscuits served between innings, assuming the first innings lasted long enough, which it usually did. There would be a smattering of spectators, generally relatives of the players, either home or visiting, and the scores were put up by hand on the board (sometimes blackboard) which had hooks on. Onto these the printed numbers on their white enamel squares could be attached, two for the batsmen, one for the team score and one for wickets – sometimes even one below that for the last man's score. If it was really sophisticated, there were two even further down to denote the bowlers by their numbers in the batting order, which was written down in the score-book. Scoring was done by hand of course, each ball bowled recorded in the overs grid, dots for no runs scored, the number if runs were scored, and a capital W for a wicket.

Later in my life, after I had dropped out of the straight life and become a *dharma* bum writing poetry and taking drugs, pot and then psychedelics (not to mention getting trepanned), my love of cricket never died. At a more advanced age, I took up village cricket again. On one occasion I went out to open the batting on a tab of acid with a glucose tablet in my mouth. The opening bowler was very fast, but I hadn't a shred of fear and played him easily. I saw the ball as large as a grapefruit and was really enjoying the experience. Unfortunately it came to a premature end when I was caught on the boundary hitting a massive six – and the fielder didn't step back over the boundary line!

Nowadays everything has to happen fast – you can't hang about for five days to get a result, which may well be a draw, oh no. It's got to be quick and decisive, so one-day games were invented, 50 overs a side – then even that was too slow, so in came 20-over games. There's no longer any time to dig in, get a good look at the bowling, play yourself in till you're seeing the ball large. There are no passengers any more, fast bowlers put out to graze at long leg or third man, even in test cricket, which is still played between all the cricket-playing nations, the fielding is now super-hot. The county championship still takes place in front of a few sleepy spectators in the pavilions with their MCC ties and blazers, but the real excitement is now in the one day game – I wonder how long the longer forms will survive?

Am I nostalgic? Not really – the game must move with the times and the skills have to be adapted to the new forms. It's an evolutionary process. Long live the game.

If I had all my time to myself, which I'm afraid I do not, I would still love to spend all day at Lords watching a test match, with sandwiches and warm beer, as John Major recalled it. I'd enjoy the odd snooze; seeing the pigeons in the outfield scattering as the ball is sent racing across grass marked with the two-tone shades of green from the mower's backwards and forwards tracks; the anticipation of the new ball when the allotted overs are bowled and that shiny red "cherry" is taken by the opening bowler.

On occasions, when driving around the countryside in summer, I still can't resist to slow down and watch if I see a game taking place on the village green. It is the quintessence of Englishness and if this Sceptred Isle has given anything of value to the rest of the world besides its incomparable language, it is surely, as Aldous Huxley perceptively noted, the invention and organisation of team games, and of those the pearl in the oyster is undoubtedly that of the flannelled fools.

Fashion

Psychedelic summer

[left] 'Eye's Eye's Fuggin Eye's' necklace made by Kiki Na Art.
Based in Ireland, she creates hand drawn and painted, bespoke jewellery, featuring icons and
bold patterns. These necklaces are made of heavy card with a bright gleaming lacquer finish.
Prices range between €85 and €160
kikinaart.com

[above] 'Insane Acidic Nirvana Lemon' T shirt by Ged Well's Insane Emporium.
Screen printed cotton T shirt. Available in small, medium, large, extra large. £29
insaneemporium.com

Pink Wave Shirtwaister dress by Eponine London
Eponine's designs feature eye catching Mediterranean and African patterns. They are made from African Cotton. This design has three-quarter-length sleeves and the skirt is pleated with hidden pockets and falls below the knee. Made in the UK.
£465
eponinelondon.com

Lucy and Yak dungarees
Made from light weight twill, available in various bold and beautiful colours.
Super comfortable, hard wearing dungarees, available in sizes 8–16.
£38
lucyandyak.com

Bedroom: The furniture is mostly from eBay. The arts and crafts spindle back chair was found on a street in New Cross. The bed is Ikea, covered with a pillow mountain. The pillows are all vintage Swedish ones – marked seconds from Howe, London. I love things more if they are imperfect. The mental 1970s blanket was on my mum's bed as a child. The bedside lamp was being chucked away by my gran.

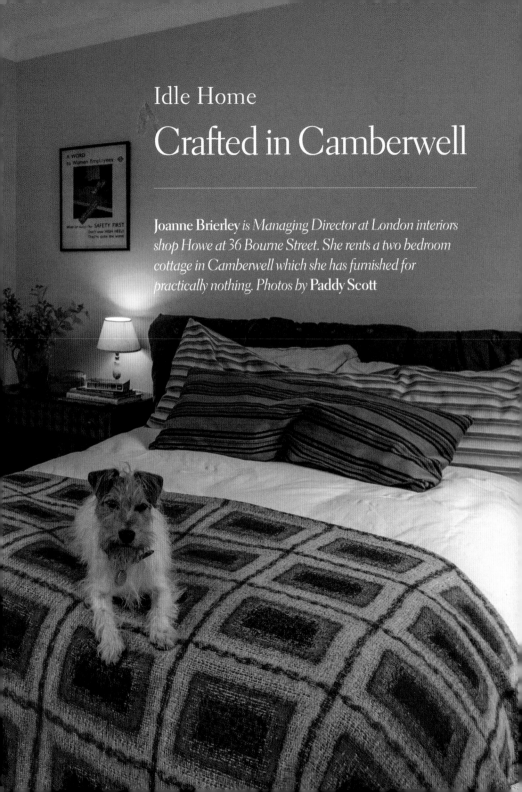

Idle Home
Crafted in Camberwell

Joanne Brierley *is Managing Director at London interiors shop Howe at 36 Bourne Street. She rents a two bedroom cottage in Camberwell which she has furnished for practically nothing. Photos by* **Paddy Scott**

I GREW up in a small semi-detached house in suburban Blackpool on a street that closely resembles Brookside Close. The unexceptional furniture was generally either from the 1970s when my parents married, or from the Argos catalogue. My parents didn't have anything old or worn as it wasn't their taste, and they never paid a great deal of attention to the house.

But interiors and furniture was a passion for me from an early age. I discovered Ikea at 13, and reading their catalogue or visiting Ikea Warrington were favourite things to do. I also used to get my dad to take my sister and me around terrible Barratt show-homes, so I could see inside other houses. I used to plan re-decorating my room, and buying new things for it, even though I knew it was a pipe dream.

I studied art and design and was certain that I would work in that world, but wasn't sure in what capacity. I only took two A-levels – art and graphic design. I discovered eBay at around 15 years old, and found a fantastically lucrative opportunity. There was a shop in Blackpool town centre that sold clothes from Topshop, Miss Selfridge, Dorothy Perkins (all Philip Green's Arcadia stores) that had been damaged in store, or were faulty. I used to buy the best pieces for very little money, such as £3 for a dress that might have been £50 new, or £7 for a leather bag which might have been £80 new. I would list them on eBay with full and frank descriptions, and sell them with no reserves. I had a knack for picking the sought-after pieces, by keeping my eye on the shops and spotting celebrities in magazines who had worn something from one

[top left] Landing: Regency chair from 1820 in foreground from a junk shop in Blackpool – £30. The rented house has an enormous ceiling mounted MDF pigeon-hole rack, on the upstairs landing, which houses all my outdoor kit and bags and shoes.

[top right] Bedroom view: Collection of vintage and old Swedish Army/Navy shirts which I often wear to work. The house looks out on to a local park. Apollo chilling in the 1930s folding dog bed I bought at Kempton antiques market.

[opposite] Living/dining room: The Edwardian screen on the far left was being thrown out by a friend in Blackpool; he had it in his home when he was a little boy and he is now 79. The floor lamp was a present to my granny from her sister for her Silver Wedding anniversary in the 1970s. The Swedish pair of chairs and Swedish Empire sofa were given to me by a friend of Christopher's. Stacks of magazines to read – no TV.

of those stores. I remember one dress that cost me £4 going for £120. I did this for a couple of years, and gave up my other part-time work. This experience gave me the ambition to work for myself, as it showed me what was possible if you have a good idea. All that money went into feeding my passion for skiing – money well spent.

I got a place at Goldsmiths in London, where I studied BA Textiles and left Blackpool at age 19.

At the start of my final year, a friend asked me what I was going to do when I finished the degree; I had no idea, and she suggested I meet her dad. She took me to the antiques and design shop HOWE on Pimlico Road – her dad is Christopher Howe. I was blown over by what I saw – there was a magical variety of stuff, from really serious, valuable and grand antiques through to mid-century and more affordable. I knew nothing about any of the furniture but I offered to help, for free, in the way I knew I could, which was take photographs of the stock and do uploading to the website, as this is

what I had been doing on eBay. I worked there without payment (very happily as I just wanted a foot in the door) twice a week for around six months, then left as I had to put all my time into my final degree show. On finishing at Goldsmiths in June 2009, I wrote Christopher an old fashioned hand-written letter asking for a job, and he obliged.

I started at Howe in July 2009 and worked for six months at his "big shop" on the Pimlico Road, very much as a junior. At Christmas time, Christopher gave me the option to try and "make something" of the small amount of leather and fabric stock he had, and make use of his "little shop" at the front of his house.

I worked alone in the little shop for five years, doing everything: selling, buying, creating new stock, book-keeping (badly!), cleaning, preparing orders, visiting clients – the lot. It was fantastic but completely exhausting. Eventually I got Emily, a recent graduate from the RCA, to help. Things picked up with two of us. We quite quickly advertised and became three. We

[top] At the shop: The current display for the nearby RHS Chelsea Flower Show. Some skins of leather out on the York stone slabs are at the front of the shop.

[opposite] Inside the shop, stacks of vintage hand-dyed linens for sale, alongside the leathers, new fabrics, and wallpaper.

are now at five, and I'm about to take us to a team of six.

Christopher is pretty hands-off day to day, as he is kept very busy working at the big shop. The last three years or so have seen the little shop really take off. We have made it into a separate company to Howe London. I feel hugely lucky to have found my niche and spend my waking hours on something I feel so passionately about. This year I turned 31 and in July this year it will be a decade since I started at Howe, as a student intern.

I've ended up with a pretty lucky set up without really designing it so. I (and all three of my other "leather girls" as we call ourselves) live in Camberwell, a brilliant part of London. My little rented two bedder houses me, and our overflow office, as the office in our shop can only seat three. We all take turns working in my house, and because we all get on so well, it works perfectly fine! Our warehouse where we keep all the vegetable tanned leather is just about 150 metres away, across the other side of the park opposite my house. When I lie in bed, I can look out of the window and see the back wall of my warehouse, and its giant disused chimney!

I generally start the day in my "home office" then pop around to the warehouse to see one of the girls who might be there preparing the latest orders. I then make my way to the shop and spend time with the girls there, and get on with a bit of work in the office or deal with some clients. My dog Apollo is with me the whole time, and together we are in control of our timetable, which is a total joy and I feel very lucky to live at my pace. Because we cycle around London, I feel like I am doing it at my own speed, and so I don't have the sensation that London is controlling me, which quite a few of my friends are suffering from. 🌀

36bournestreet.com

[top] Home office (at the back of the house, blissfully quiet): piles of vintage fabrics that we are working on recreating in Northern mills, and an iMac for all the emails and admin. I usually spend the first few early hours of the day in here, most often in pyjamas with a massive mug of tea with BBC6 Music on.

[opposite] Back yard: One of my many bikes. I'm growing salad leaves, herbs and yellow cherry tomatoes this year. The heavily carved side table is from eBay. The folding metal table is a prototype from Howe London. The cast iron table was a street find in Belgravia.

Art flâneur
Physical graffiti

Tim Richardson *investigates a cult-like sect of Victorians in deceptively leafy Surrey but is not so impressed by a* Theatre of the Natural World *in Whitechapel*

SURREY is one of those commuter-belt counties derided by metropolitans and "real" country-dwellers as gin-and-Jag territory, where stockbrokers kiss goodbye to their bored wives each morning and pop in to the golf club on the way home. Yet, taken by the square mile, Surrey counts as the most densely-wooded county in England. Like those other vilified Home counties, Berkshire, Hampshire, Hertfordshire and Buckinghamshire, its deep-cut lanes and gentle wooded vales have long been a source of inspiration to artists and poets.

In the 1880s there was a whole Surrey school of country-cottage artists led by Helen Allingham who revelled in country flowers such as campanulas, wallflowers and geraniums, while the Arts and Crafts movement found perhaps its most successful expression here, in the houses and gardens created by the Edwardian planting designer Gertrude Jekyll and architect Edwin Lutyens. Jekyll's first book was entitled *Old West Surrey* – I love the particularity of *West* Surrey (speaking as an *East* Berkshire man) – in which she chronicled minutiae such as the different kinds of gates, stiles and doors that she came across in the lanes. Victorian poets and novelists were also attracted to this shy and bucolic county, which seems to hide its riches beneath a veil of greenery: Tennyson and George Eliot lived at Haslemere, and George Meredith at Box Hill.

The Watts Gallery in the village

George Frederic Watts, *Physical Energy*, 1881–1904. Gesso grosso. Watts Gallery Trust of Compton, just off the A3, seems emblematic of Surrey's double-life: the stockings and suspenders worn beneath the stockbroker's pinstripe. George Frederick Watts was an outrageously ambitious High Victorian painter and sculptor who genuinely believed that his art had the potential to alter the universe and our perception of it. This gallery, set in a purpose-built Arts and Crafts building that he commissioned, stands as a shrine to his unique style of symbolist painting and sculpture.

"Shrine" is an overused word, but seems apposite here, because there is something ever-so-slightly cultish about Watts. A religiose fug enfolds the chapel-like building. Which makes it all the more delightful that the gallery itself is overseen not by wild-eyed cultists but smartly turned-out ladies and gentlemen of the locality, dispensing helpful directions in the galleries and fudge in the gift-shop. David Koresh got it wrong in so many ways.

I was prompted to visit the gallery again because of the presence of a new cast of *Physical Energy* (1904), Watts' monumental bronze sculpture of a rearing horse and waving rider, positioned for six months in the forecourt of the Royal Academy at Somerset House, as it was when it was first shown to the public during the Summer Exhibition of that year. Judging by contemporary photographs, it was a more affecting ensemble back then, when the forecourt had a uniform surface of sandy gravel and the sculpture base was a simple, abstract plinth rather than the distracting dry-stone wall effect of today's version (not to mention the Portakabin ticket office and bog-standard shiny metal café chairs). This new cast is now back in Surrey.

The wholly Victorian admixture of sturdy figurative expression and vaunting spiritual allegory found in *Physical Energy* typifies Watts' *oeuvre*. It has made him one of those difficult artists who catch something of the spirit of their age and become massive celebrities – but then slowly sink, weighed down by the condescension of critics and historians who cannot forgive the inbuilt anachronism of the work. In Watts' case this arises because of the apparent indigestibility of his moralistic vision and the symbolic excesses of his super-sized canvases and sculptures, which he constantly reworked. Accustomed as we are to lashings of irony in contemporary art, the very idea of the philosopher-painter – whose formative artistic experience was a visit to the Sistine Chapel – will turn many a modern stomach.

In the gallery, some of the symbolist works might indeed appear somewhat dauby to modern eyes, with gaseous or "vaporescent" (as Ruskin called it) forms swirling around fraught-looking figures from myth or the Bible. But there are some truly memorable paintings, too.

The Minotaur (1885) is a remarkable work depicting the bull-like beast half-turned away, looking out to sea. It was inspired by news reports of underage Irish girls being procured for prostitution as they disembarked at the London docks (bearing in mind that the legal age of consent at this time was 13: they were even younger than that). The casual, human-like pose of the beast is chilling enough, but the masterstroke is the calm evening sky and the smooth stone of the balustrade against which it rests. The juxtaposition seems to encapsulate Victorian hypocrisy. If you look closely enough, you can see the small bird crushed in the minotaur's hand.

The highlight of the gallery is the great *Eve Trilogy* (1893-1903), of which the third panel, *Eve Repentant*, is the most extraordinary. Eve is turned away from us, her long golden tresses following the arc of her back. She is blurry, indistinct, almost ectoplasmic, burying her face in the forest, the leaves enfolding and clasping her. The darkness of Watts' canvases and the indistinctness of his forms make

his paintings all too easy to bypass in the many municipal galleries where his works hang. But close attention, as here, reveals a sensuous, simmering quality and an explosive inner drama.

My own feeling was that Watts was electrified by women all his life. This can be seen in his portraits, which are frankly admiring of women without ever descending into lechery. His depiction of Lillie Langtry must be one of the most sexually charged portraits ever produced. Watts' men are dull by comparison – even Swinburne looks a bore. GK Chesterton, who wrote a whole book on Watts, put it more delicately, observing that he cultivated, "a worship of great men so complete that it makes him tend in the direction of painting them all alike".

A visit to the Whitechapel Gallery and Mark Dion's *Theatre of the Natural World* was necessary to reinstate contemporary levels of irony in the bloodstream. The main room consisted of a series of four intricately furnished hunting hides, resembling watch towers, together with emblazoned pennants, the whole ensemble entitled *The Hunting Blinds and Hunting Standards* (2005–08). The hide named "The Glutton", for example, consisted of a dining table smartly laid for a huntsman's luncheon – it had that *Marie Celeste* feel that the guests were about to arrive, or had just departed – and was reminiscent of site-specific theatre pieces where audience members are left to wander around on their own, discovering the deserted settings for the intermittent action of the play. Indeed, all of Dion's installations emanate that sense of implied or impending performance.

A new work was *The Library for the Birds of London* (2018) which comprised an aviary of finches living among a decomposing library of natural history books, while upstairs could be found two gigantic bespoke cabinets containing artefacts found in the Thames during a collaborative art action. Drawers could be smoothly pulled out to reveal carefully labelled cassette tapes, babies' dummies, combs, mobile phone accessories, old toothbrushes, mirrors, balls and a surprising number of coconuts. The set-up was reminiscent of the Pitt Rivers Museum in Oxford, where you might open a drawer to find a shrunken head.

Dion's work is about ways of engaging with the world – principally through the rituals of scientific collection and analysis. He is fascinated by the accoutrements of science: the uniforms, the equipment, even the furniture. Many of his works

indulge in mock taxonomy (the discipline of classification) and he has published numerous books which formalise the work in similar fashion. In his early work he succumbed to the facetious irony of using kitsch (in his case, Disney tropes). I confess that I find his artistic version of scientific endeavour considerably less interesting than the activities of actual scientists such as Sir Thomas Browne an Hans Sloane, and experiencing his installations is nothing like as exciting as, say, standing in Darwin's study at Down House, in Kent. As such I find Dion's work diverting but never profound.

If one is tempted to label all conceptual art facetious and shallow, then a visit to the Joan Jonas retrospective at Tate Modern (until August 5) will perhaps dispel that notion. Artists are constantly being falsely labelled by curators as "pioneers" of artistic genres such as installation, film and performance (Dion included), but in Jonas's case this is incontestably true. Her performance pieces in the 1960s and 1970s, as well as her recent work, are magnificently *avant garde*. Some of them also prove magnificently indigestible in a gallery setting.

With the early perfomances, it seems you really had to be there – gazing at a mock-up of a

[Above] Joan Jonas, *The Juniper Tree*, 1976/1994. Installation – 24 works on silk, acrylic paint, wooden structure, string of 29 wooden balls, ladder, kimono, mirror, glass jars, 78 slides, box and other materials. Overall display dimensions variable. Tate, purchased 2008. Wilkinson Gallery, London, 2008. Installation view photos by Seraphina Nevill. © 2018 Joan Jonas : Artists Rights Society (ARS), New York : DACS, London.

handmade set for *The Juniper Tree* (1976) and grainy footage of a SoHo loft on an adjacent TV monitor is no substitute for the real thing. You have to admire the Tate's chutzpah in attempting this at all. The final rooms of this appropriately overblown show do give us "real" renditions of recent film/installation works such as *Stream or River, Flight or Pattern* (2016–17). This piece includes footage of a Saigon street, a bird sanctuary in Singapore and a subterranean mausoleum in Genoa. 🐌

PREVIEW
Flâneur recommends

Greta Schödl & Tomaso Binga: Vocalising
Fascinating work consisting of repetitive text and symbols.
Until July 14
Richard Saltoun Gallery, 41 Dover Street, London W1S 4NS

Edward Bawden
Until September 9
Welcome survey of the very British printmaker and watercolourist.
Dulwich Picture Gallery, Gallery Road, London SE21 7AD

Aftermath: Art in the Wake of World War One
Reassuringly internationalist survey including Grosz, Masson and Picasso.
Until September 16
Tate Britain, Millbank, London SW1P 4RG

Books

Bedtime for democracy?

Cathleen Mair finds it hard to drift off on a lumpy mattress, gliding down a canal in the middle of a forest, with reams of political thinking to hand…

Goodnight Sweetheart: A Miscellany of Morose, Misanthropic Middle-Aged Musings and Mattresses, **Anil Mistry** and friends (self-published, £14)

As he gets older, photographer Anil Mistry finds himself identifying with saggy, stained mattresses, abandoned along the side of the road. He has spent the past three years photographing ones he's found down various dingy side streets, leaning against lamp posts or dumped in rubbish skips. *Goodnight Sweetheart* presents these photographs alongside poems and reflections by some of his male friends – sullen mattress-inspired musings on aging, modern life and the inevitable decay that awaits us all. "I've always been grumpy," writes one contributor. "Now I have the perfect excuse." It's an

amusing, thoughtful and sometimes moving compendium, and all profits go to CALM (Campaign Against Living Miserably), who undertake very laudable work to prevent male suicide.

This Book Will Send You to Sleep, **Professor K McCoy and Dr Hardwick** (Ebury, £9.99)

"Each page is guaranteed to be devoid of excitement," promise Prof McCoy and Dr Hardwick in this little volume's introduction. In writing the most boring book possible, the authors sought to strike the perfect balance between pointless fact and tedious sentences. Rather than stimulating you, it should lull the mind into a state of dreamy, sleepy disinterest, perfect for nodding off.

The chapters are short and dense, with subjects ranging from the taxonomy of molluscs to the history of the Lithuanian monarchy and facts about roundabouts. However, while most chapters are indeed extremely dull, I actually found myself rather intrigued by some. Particularly enjoyable was a chapter on the dullest entries in interesting diaries: "Lay long abed", wrote Samuel Pepys in 1660. An entry from Wittgenstein's diary reads as follows: "Sat watching clouds drift slowly past the window. Then fell asleep." Days well spent, say we at the *Idler*.

The Communist Manifesto
by Karl Marx and Friedrich Engels,
adapted by **Martin Rowson**
(Self Made Hero, £12.99)
   This year marks the 200th anniversary of Karl Marx's birth, and 170 years since *The Communist Manifesto* was first published, yet the political thinker's relevance shows no signs of abating. As satirical cartoonist Martin Rowson points out, when just 43 individuals possess as much wealth as half of the rest of us, Marx still has a lot left to say. Published in 1848, and written hastily over the course of a weekend in Brussels, the *Communist Manifesto* remains the most influential, and perhaps the most lucid, introduction to communism and Marx's understanding of historical materialism and class struggle. The first part of Rowson's comic adaptation, which lays out Marx's concept of class struggle in the modern industrial age, is particularly striking. It follows a bearded Marx, cigar in hand, and Engels through a dark and nightmarish landscape where demonic steel machines grind up defenseless proletarians to feed the giant and greedy capitalist monster. Witty, lively and irreverent, Rowson's graphic novel is an excellent guide to the manifesto.

Water Ways:
A Thousand Miles
Along Britain's
Canals, **Jasper Winn**
(Profile Books, £12.99)
   The *Idler* office sits along the Great Union Canal, which stretches from London to Birmingham, and offers a welcome respite from the computer on a lunch break. In fact, most people in Britain live within five miles of a canal and thanks to campaigning from activists and latterly the Canal and River Trust, this network of "slow highways" has been preserved for us to enjoy. Jasper Winn, writer in residence at the Trust, spent roughly a year

traveling along canals in England and Wales – by foot, by bike, in a kayak and by narrowboat – documenting the wildlife, history and people who have made the waterways their home. Along his travels, he encounters a "welcoming community of boaters" among whom is Kate Saffin, a member of the canal-based Alarum Theatre Company, touring a play called *Idle Women*. It tells the story of women who signed up as trainees on idle canal boats during WWII, transporting essential supplies and keeping the boats running. The play highlights one of the crucial ways in which canals formed the backbone of industry for many years. Since the 1940s, canals are no longer required for industrial purposes but, as Winn's gentle and slow book reminds us, they clearly offer a much-needed escape from our fast-paced world.

A Wood of One's Own, **Ruth Pavey** (Duckworth Overlook, £14.99)

In the late 1990s, tired of London and city life, Ruth Pavey bought four acres of land, at auction, in the Somerset Levels in the West Country and set out to plant a wood, one tree at a time. She acquired an old Rollalong, a mobile site cabin, from her neighbour, a retired farmer called Ted, so she could sleep in the wood while working – not quite as romantic as it sounds, as winter nights are long and cold, and the cabin only small. This is where Pavey is at her best: self-deprecating, unpretentious and not ashamed to let you know she eventually gave up on the Rollalong, buying a cottage in nearby Langport instead. *A Wood of One's Own* is a delightful memoir; it draws you in with gentle humour, loving descriptions of the land and locals, and Pavey's gorgeous illustrations.

Room to Dream, **David Lynch and Kristine McKenna** (Canongate, £25)

When *Twin Peaks* returned to screens last year, following a 25 year hiatus, it caused quite a stir, and viewers, myself included, spent weeks trying to dissect the show's strange and unexpected twists and turns. Now fans have the opportunity to get inside its co-creator's head. David Lynch, visionary director of *Mulholland Drive* and *Blue Velvet* fame, has been called "the most important director of this era" by the *Guardian*, and *Room to Dream* certainly does his extraordinary creative career justice. Part memoir, part biography, it tells the story of Lynch's life from two perspectives: one based on journalist Kristine McKenna's interviews with the film-maker's friends, family members and colleagues including Peggy Reaves, his first wife, and actress Isabella Rossellini, the other based on Lynch's personal reflections. It's a fitting approach to take, one that plays with memory, form and narrative in a way that reflects Lynch's films. A brilliant insight into his creative process, revealing an artist completely and wholly absorbed by his work, *Room to Dream* also sheds a light on the difficulties Lynch faced bringing projects to fruition. More surprising perhaps, is what we learn about life in the US in the 1950s and 1960s, through descriptions of Lynch's idyllic childhood, skiing and shooting squirrels in Idaho, contrasting with his days as an art student in 1960s Philadelphia, a dark and dangerous city, rife with crime, poverty and racial tensions.

A Honeybee Heart Has Five Openings: A Year of Keeping Bees, **Helen Jukes** (Scribner, £14.99)

Exhausted, stressed and struggling to settle into a new job, Helen Jukes needs a change. Then a friend gives her a colony of honeybees, and so begins a year-long foray into beekeeping. She

finds there is something about beekeeping that makes her see the world differently, makes her feel more in touch: "There does seem to be something about beekeeping that *gets in*," she writes. "I've met beekeepers who talk about *getting the bug*, that it gets *under your skin*." We learn alongside Jukes, getting to know the delicate and complex hive eco-system, delving into the history of beekeeping, reading stories on the subject from Aristotle to Eva Crane, exploring different practices of honey-gathering, mead making and wax collecting. It's a personal journey, but we are invited to share in the beautifully intimate and caring relationship she builds with the honeybees in her garden – a wonderfully warm, inspiring and human book.

How Democracy Ends, **David Runciman** (Profile, £14.99)

All things must come to an end and so too must democracy. Political scientist David Runciman explores what such an end might look like in societies where faith in democracy is firmly established, like Britain or the United States. In these cases, we may have grown so accustomed to trusting democratic

processes, like elections and a free press, that we do not notice when they no longer work. This is the real crisis of democracy, according to Runciman. The language of failed states simply doesn't describe a society like the United States: there will be no conflict, no tanks in the streets, no generals on television announcing that order has been restored. In other words, "Democracy could fail while remaining intact". In *How Democracy Ends*, Runciman probes this thesis in sharp and interesting ways. The chapter on the impact of digital technologies, big data and online surveillance is particularly refreshing. While he points to some of the potential technological threats to democracy, he is keen not to overstate the influence of Facebook and "fake news" – "A lot of what Cambridge Analytica is selling is simply hot air" – and suggests that manipulating an electorate is a lot more difficult than it looks.

Notting Hill: A Walking Guide by **Julian Mash** (Notting Hill Editions, £14.99)
This walking guide, beautifully bound and typeset by the excellent folk at Notting Hill Editions, is presented as an "antidote to the iPhone", a book that will make you look up from your screen and actually see the world around you, maybe even meet people. Across four rambling walks through the West London neighbourhood, author Julian Mash takes in Portobello Market, the Notting Hill Carnival, record stores, bookshops, *pasteis de nata* and Labour MP Tony Benn's former home. It's a gentle, rambling jaunt through the area's rich literary, musical and political history packed with curious facts and local recommendations. Did you know, for instance, that writer Ian Fleming so loathed Modernism, he named one of James Bond's arch villains after the architect who designed the Trellick Tower, Erno Goldfinger? All in all, a lovely little book. 🐌

Small press

We're all doomed. Not.

David Collard *says the novel's not dead and nor is indie publishing*

Here's novelist and provocateur Will Self: "I think the novel is absolutely doomed to become a marginal cultural form, along with easel painting and the classical symphony. And that's already happened."

With a new novel to promote, Self recycled this familiar spiel in the *Guardian* earlier this year. Warming to his theme he went on: "It's impossible to think of a novel that's been a water-cooler moment in England, or in Britain, since *Trainspotting*, probably." He then demolishes any claim he might make for expertise in the matter by stating: "I don't tend to read contemporary fiction much; I think I'm going to take a bit of a furlough from writing fiction in order to look at fiction a bit more."

Mr Self could start with this year's Republic of Consciousness Prize shortlist. (I wrote about the long list in a previous issue of the *Idler* – 13 remarkable books, none of which will prompt water-cooler moments, but then neither did *Mrs Dalloway*.) These thirteen were whittled down to a short list of six, as follows:

Ariana Harwicz, *Die, My Love* (Charco Press)
David Hayden, *Darker with the Lights On* (Little Island Press)
Noémi Lefebvre, *Blue Self Portrait* (Les Fugitives)
Preti Taneja, *We That Are Young* (Galley Beggar Press)
Eley Williams, *Attrib. and other stories* (Influx Press)
Isabel Waidner, *Gaudy Bauble* (Dostoyevsky Wannabe Original)

Five of these are written by women. Here's Self again: "I'm teaching a course on the importance of literary influence and the books that influenced me as a writer, and one of my students pointed out they're all by men."

Never too late to join the party,

Will. Two of these books (by Harwicz and Lefebvre) appeared in English for the first time; four were debuts (Hayden, Taneja, Williams and Waidner). A week after Self's piece appeared, this cohort of talents gathered with their publishers at the University of Westminster's Fyvie Hall for the prize-giving shindig.

The prize's founder, Neil Griffiths, began by announcing a special *hors concours* prize: "The William Gass award for metafiction and for being the best person in publishing, like ever". This went to the poet, novelist and publisher Charles Boyle who has for the past ten years run small publisher CB Editions single-handedly from his west London home, managing the best backlist of any indie publisher. Last year Charles took time out to publish two books under his occasional pen-name Jack Robinson: one (entitled *Robinson*) a pungent response to the Brexit Referendum and the other, *An Overcoat*, a dazzling riff on the life and work of Stendhal. Reviewing this in the *Guardian* Nick Lezard said: "I read it with an idiot grin, delighted by every sentence, each of which has been constructed with remarkable care, not just for its own sound and plausibility, but to reflect the daily realities of life … I can't think of a wittier, more engaging, stylistically audacious, attentive and generous writer working in the English language right now."

The outright winner came as no surprise: *Attrib.* by Eley Williams – a debut collection of short stories. Hard to describe or summarise, 17 thoughtfully-wrought tales explore language and life and (quite often) the aftermath of separation in prose that is deft, playful, light-footed and richly satisfying. She is also extremely funny: in "Foley" a recording expert, contracted to provide sound effects on a museum tape to accompany an art

exhibition, is acutely aware of the many background sounds in her house – a distant cat flap goes "pyongyang" while a faulty radiator mutters to itself: "Sissinghurst. Sissinghurst and gourd".

Eley Williams is formidably gifted, a fully-formed talent.

Her publisher, Influx Press, was co-founded in 2012 by the writer and editor Kit Caless who is, among many other things, the author of *Spoon's Carpets: An Appreciation*, an engaging monograph dedicated to the floorings of the Weatherspoons pub chain. He and Assistant Editor Sanya Semakula aim to publish four books a year and their current list consists of 18 titles. You'll certainly want to invest in a copy of *Attrib.* (and all the other Republic of Consciousness titles), but here are four more recommendations, three of them non-fiction, which you can order direct from Influx.

Twenty-odd writers contribute to *An Unreliable Guide to London* including the great M John Harrison; Paul Ewen (whose *Francis Plug: How to Be a Public Author* (Galley Beggar Press), is one of the funniest novels I've ever read) and Eley Williams (again).

Signal Failure is an account by the author Tom Jeffreys of a journey on foot from London to Birmingham following the route of the proposed HS2 rail link, a downbeat exercise in psychogeography and a snapshot of Brexit Britain.

Paul Scraton's *Ghosts on the Shore* is about the behemoth summer camps erected by the Nazis in the late 1930s on the Baltic island island of Rügen, featured a few years ago by Jonathan Meades in his excellent telly programme *Jerry Building*. They are now being refurbished as slightly sinister luxury apartments.

Finally, if you want to get down with the kids *Hold Tight* by Jeffrey Boakye is "the definitive book on grime and modern black British music culture". If, like me, you've never been more than dimly aware of Dizzee Rascal, Kano, Lethal Bizzle and the really excellent Stormzy, this is the place to start.

Back to the Republic of Consciousness Prize. I've now read all the shortlisted books and recommend them without

exception, although some exercise a more immediate appeal than others. Take a punt. Each of them will put the snap in your celery or raise your hackles, and ideally both. Or you could splash out on Will Self's latest, which isn't half bad. ◉

littleislandpress.co.uk
cbeditions.com
sadpresspoetry.wordpress.com
influxpress.com
andotherstories.org
dalkeyarchive.com

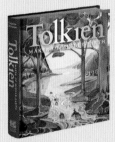

Craft

Blue is beautiful

Ros Badger *gets inspired by the florals of Anna Atkins cyanotype photography*

When I first saw *Photographs of British Algae: Cyanotype Impressions*, at the British Library, Anna Atkins' surprisingly modern-looking Prussian Blue "photogenic drawings" I felt a sense of awe at the beauty of her work, a similar feeling to when I was introduced to the photographic work of Karl Blossfeldt.

Anna Atkins developed her interest in cyanotype photography as a means of recording botanical specimens for a reference book. As a botanist and illustrator, Atkins wanted to record as many interesting floral species as possible. She had met William Henry Fox Talbot, the creator of "photograms", the process that used chemicals and sunlight to create images on paper, through her father. Talbot's discovery led to the development of the camera and Anna had also been introduced to Sir John Herschel, the accidental inventor of the cyanotype printing method.

Both Blosfeldt and Atkins recognised profound beauty in nature's forms Blosfeldt, who worked in the late 19th century, said that "the plant must be valued as a totally artistic and architectural structure". His photographic images of plants were originally produced as teaching material, made using a homemade camera that could magnify the subject up to 30 times and transforming the subjects into art images in the same way that Atkins's blue print impressions of seaweed and ferns transcend from her initial intention of documenting nature into beautiful creative visual forms.

Atkins continued her love of the cyanotype process with making *Cyanotypes of British and Foreign Ferns* (1853) and *Cyanotypes of British and Foreign Flowering Plants and Ferns*. The images form these books having a timeless appeal to nature lovers and artists alike.

The visual transmutation and the alchemical nature of the cyanotype process is what attracts me. So I have found out more about the process so that I can create my own visual impressions. It is really rather simple and very addictive!

Creating a Cyanotype

Also known as sun printing, the chemical liquid only becomes "live" when the two elements, ferric ammonium citrate and potassium ferricyanide, are mixed with water and blended together to make a 50/50 acid yellow solution. Only then is the mixture UV light sensitive.

The solution can be used to coat paper or fabric and once the surface is dry, anything that is placed onto it and exposed to UV light will, once rinsed with clear water, leave a bleached out silhouette against the Prussian blue surface.

As well as working with plain cartridge and watercolour papers I have tried coating old printed paper surfaces, like pre-printed pages and handwritten sheets from old exercise books, to add another interesting layer to the process and I find this works very well.

You will need:

Ferric ammonium citrate and potassium ferricyanide. These come in crystal form and are easily available at photographic suppliers or online.

100g of each will get you started.
Two small mixing vessels bowls
   or jam jars
Weighing scales
A measuring jug
A brown or green wine bottle
Old spoon
The chemicals can stain so cover surfaces and use rubber gloves and wear an apron.

Mixing the chemicals

Dilute the two chemicals separately by mixing 25 grams ferric ammonium citrate with 100 ml water and 10 grams potassium ferricyanide with 100 ml water.

Stir each until the powdered crystals dissolve.

Mix equal quantities of each solution together in a third container and store this in a brown or green jar or bottle. An old wine bottle and cork works well, but don't forget to label it!

The solution should be stored in a cupboard or store room not in direct light.

To make a cyanotype print
Coat your paper or fabric with the yellow solution using a paint brush or sponge.

Once coated, leave it to dry in a dark place. I made a tent-shaped frame from a cardboard box and used a dustbin liner to cover any cracks.

Once dry you can keep the paper in a dark envelope, bag or box, it should remain sensitive for a number of months as long as it isn't exposed to UV.

Place your chosen leaf, flower or object onto the coated paper or fabric. Then sandwich this with a piece of glass and expose it to UV light. Sunlight is the traditional source, but UV lamps also work.

Experiment with exposure times but if the sun is bright you will see the colour change within minutes.

Take the paper and rinse in cold water until the silhouette is free of the yellow solution and the water runs clear. Oxidation is also hastened this way – bringing out the intense blue. Place on a dry flat surface to dry.

Exposure times can vary from minutes to hours, depending on light intensity, and no two prints seem the same but all this is part of the attraction of this process for me. Adding bleach to the final rinse can make the blue darker and experimenting by brushing a 50/50 bleach water solution around the edge of the image can add a shadow effect. 🐌

Music

Erland Cooper

Tom Hodgkinson meets the Scottish musician whose new album, Solan
Goose, *is a mesmerising piece of work which sits somewhere between
classical and electronic, and is inspired by his native Orkney*

*You are from Orkney but live
in London. Do you miss the
wilder places?*
Yes, very much. I think
reconnecting with nature or
landscape is one clear way to
find a genuine peace. Albeit for a
short time.

Who's that bird on your hand?
That is Ragnar Lodbrok. He's not a
Peregrine falcon native to Orkney
but a rescue bird, I was told. I've
mixed views on birds of prey in
captivity. At Bay of Skaill I had to
see for myself before passing
judgment. Sanctuary and
conservation are important. These
birds were fed and flown several
times daily and adored by their
keepers. However, seeing into the
eyes of the fastest animal on the
planet was quite humbling. The
falcon is a truly astonishing bird.

*When was true last time you had a
proper job and what was it?*
I work 12–15 hour days in several
jobs I won't bore you with, but any
spare time I have, when I'm not
producing, writing or mixing for
other projects or artists, I make
music for myself. Despite
limitations with my time, I hope
I'm still making as much music as
my current peers. I try to be
militant with the time I have to
create, which usually involves me
working at my best around dawn
chorus time.

We've heard Solan Goose *which is
lovely. Where and how did you write
this album?*
Thank you. I wrote this the day
after watching Jóhann
Jóhannsson perform at the
Barbican. I went to the studio
around 7am. The road noise and
building works around me were

Erland with friend Ragnar Lodbrok:
"Seeing into the eyes of the fastest animal on the planet was quite humbling."

hammering in a particular key. I replicated that into a humming drone on a synth through tape and then improvised the first melody I played on the piano. Those seven notes landed so I recorded them over two chords. I named the file, Gannet. I started a mix session for someone else, then did a writing session with some young buck, then another mix for someone else and left at rush hour. When I got back on the tube, I tried to remember the Orcadian name for Gannet to distract me. Eventually when I returned to the studio, I did another layer, renamed the track to its Orcadian counterpart and kept moving on that way over a few weeks, until it was finished and could nest more contently with some others.

And what can you tell us about the rest of the album?
For the most part, each of the songs on the album started as an improvised piece like that, recording piano alone or perhaps writing over an ambient layer, created out of experimenting with a new sound or signal chain, usually that analogue synth fed through tape echo. Sometimes, it's good to start from nothing. I always find that something will come and if it doesn't, my head is thinking too deeply about other more practical

things. If a melody arrives and then I forget it, I'm confident another will drop in to replace it, or it will come back bolder and stronger. Sometimes just silence and the soft felt hammers from the piano, after a period of loud noise from outside, were enough to write but other times, experimental layers with their unplanned harmonics were better. I also really value sleep melody. "Cattie-face" was co-written in my sleep with Simon Tong, a melody he had discarded almost a decade previously. He couldn't remember it when I played it to him.

How important is idling to you?
Given the chance, I could happily stare out of a window for an hour and go deep into a 100 mile stare. In truth I don't get enough of it, advice welcome. It's like spotting a rare bird for me after trekking the cliffs for days to find it among a large colony all along, laughing away with its mates at how easy it really all is.

What are you listening to right now?
I always seem to fly back to Julianna Barwick's *Nepenthe* or Jon Hopkins' *Immunity* via Cluster's *Zuckerziet* and a Clint Mansell score.

Can we see you out and about on the road this summer?
Yes, I'm surprised to say I'm playing four festivals this year with Solan Goose. Unexpected for a record I didn't plan on releasing commercially, rather keeping to myself or close friends to distract and encourage more idling. 🐌

Erland plays the Caught by the River Stage at the Port Eliot Festival, 29 July, and the Good Life Experience, 15 September, plus more to be announced. erlandcooper.com

The sound of the stones: Erland finds the right frequency

Music

Heaven knows I'm mithering now

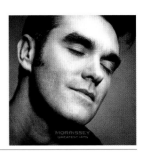

Jonnie Bayfield *mounts an unfashionable defence of Manchester's most miserable and maligned son*

BEFORE Christmas, the now almost universally reviled Morrissey released his 11th solo album, *Low In High School*. Now, I must confess that I, like many other aficionados, have felt for years like a Sunday league mother, gathered by the sidelines, looking on at the playing field while our boy frequently trips on his own ankle, scores own-goals, and feigns asthma attacks.

If the great man is not publicly comparing seal culling to the Holocaust, he's calling the Chinese a "subspecies" because of their treatment of animals, or bleating on about the antiquated monarchy (the latter of which I once could have agreed if it wasn't for Princess Margaret's hypnotic chain-smoking in Netflix's *The Crown*). As recently as April, he openly endorsed the far right, anti-Islam minority party For Britain, whose views seem to be in direct opposition to most of the

prevailing thought in *Low In High School*, particularly with regard to our Armed Forces. Confusing.

However, like all good sons, Morrissey does not listen to his devoted mothers shouting desperate love over a bitter wind. He knows better than us, and has, intentionally or not, set about turning his life and work into a walking, crooning art installation of blistering effect and difficult – but ultimately extraordinary – brilliance.

In itself, *Low In High School* is symbolic of the great man's final stage transition into full polarisation mode. Recent years have not been kind to the former Smiths' frontman, and, along with his record label battles, he has become as reviled by the tabloids as fact-checking or Jeremy Corbyn's suspiciously Russian-looking hat.

Musically he soldiers on and stands alone. This record shifts him

courageously into the realm of protest song. Though outwardly it would seem that he now has more in common with Roy Harper or Bob Dylan, Morrissey is operating through the looking glass of the counter-culture's usual left wing concerns. The "unheard" voices with which Morrissey sympathises rise from an increasingly dark and politically taboo place.

The album itself begins as you'd expect: with the sound of a man screaming into a void. "Teach your kids to recognise and despise all the propaganda/Filtered down by the dead echelons mainstream media," are the beleaguered entertainer's opening lines. Not only is "My Love I'd Do Anything For You" a perfect summation of the entire *Low In High School* experience, it's also a pretty good encapsulation of the Twitterverse: the torrents of content and cul-de-sac of deafening discourse.

From this we fall like rain into the brilliant double espresso of bitterness that is "I Wish You Lonely", a classic Moz conceit of rage and despair, directed at all who have wronged humanity. "Tombs are full of fools who gave their life upon command/Of monarchy, oligarch, head of state,

potentate," he shouts down the can with characteristic scorn. But the reason for the curse of the title? "So that you might see routine for me/ Since the day I was born." It makes you wonder how he can bring himself to carry on.

This well of vitriol toward those in authority brings me to a personal favourite, "I Bury The Living", where Morrissey continues his tirade against the armed forces. Contentious though the song has been, is it any more disrespectful to the lives of young recruits than those fetishistic Territorial Army TV ads colouring warfare as some kind of "James Bond goes to the Halfmoon Festival" experience? Morrissey makes a hard stand, sluiced through with black humour: "Give me an order I'll blow up a border. Give me an order and I'll blow up your daughter," being a perfect example of a writer now perching uneasily on the edge of absurdity.

Along with the aggressive challenges on this album lies more easily-palatable fare: "Spent the Day in Bed" received heavy airplay upon release thanks to the jaunty pop tones and synth jingles created by producer Joe Chiccarelli and the unerring groove of stalwart guitarist Boz Boorer. It's a welcome return of a more playful frontman, which carries on through into the almost perfect Vintage Moz of "Jacky's

Only Happy When She's Up On The Stage".

With the second half of the album, we lose some venom, and thus a child's portion of interest –

I like my Morrissey hard and fast – until we reach the final track "Israel", the one that has stirred the most controversy in the "dead echelons of mainstream media" for it's sympathy for the bedevilled Jewish state, with left-leaning critics lining up to deliver Morrissey a kicking for it. Whatever you think about his politics, as a song alone this is delicate, lyrically beautiful and delivered in the most red velvet voice of the man's career.

In all, *Low In High School* is as provocative and barbed as you would hope from a Morrissey album. It is also brilliantly listenable to, and potentially one of the only musical offerings around that will make you gasp, laugh, contemplate and hate all in one sitting. In short, listening to it is like being gently throttled during the act of making love; delightful discomfort. I speak from experience.

Jonnie's picks from now…

The Low Anthem *The Salt Doll Went To Measure The Depth Of The Sea.* Tramadol folk. Ambient and absorbing nursery rhymes from the depths of hell. Good for eating with, or when putting down a beloved pet.

Chas & Dave *A Little Bit Of Us* First studio album in 30 years from national treasures. A treat for the ears. Like sitting in an unreconstructed pub listening to two old boys at the bar slowly drink their way through their own half truths.

and then…

Van Morrison *Astral Weeks* From 1968: hippy-dippy in a *Wicker Man* creepy folk song way. Like a painting we only get to hear. Best served stoned.

Eurythmics *Revenge* From 1986: Upbeat album best served dancing. Underrated track, "When Tomorrow Comes" is the perfect evangelist's funeral song, and shows Lennox's lyrics at their best. 🍥

@JonnieBayfield

Television
Bad timing

Not many new comedies are hitting the spot, says **Kate Bernard**, *but* Patrick Melrose *is funny*

A T dinner, many years ago, a noted wit turned to me and asked, "So, what *is* the secret of comedy? " Bemused and flattered (for it was Stephen Fry and I was young and in awe), I'd barely begun to reply when he boomed: "Timing!"

If you've only seen him as a subversive teddy-bear on *QI*, you can catch Fry's comic timing any time – *Jeeves and Wooster, A Little Bit of Fry and Laurie, Blackadder* – as an increasing number of channels apparently exist to support our dewy-eyed sentiment over classic British comedy of the last 30 years. Some – *The Fast Show, Father Ted, Peep Show* – bear repetition better than most, but one must respect Dave Allen, dour master of Irish Catholic humour, in not allowing his output to be repeated more than once.

Heaps of new comedies are screened every year yet so few really hit the spot. *This Country* (BBC iPlayer), is an exception. After two series of the mockumentary set in the council houses of a Gloucester village, Kerry's mum is the only screen legend I can think of who remains invisible. Like all good comedy *TC* has an appeal that crosses cultures and the social ABC.

Cunk on Britain (BBC2) is another mockumentary, a satire on history programme-making from Charlie Brooker which just failed to catch the breeze despite the obvious talents of Philomena Cunk, *aka* Diane Morgan. Its rapid descent into prurience, a common post-watershed crevasse, made matters predictable all too soon, and one show was enough.

The Bafta-winning *Mum* (BBC2) is what the late Terry-Thomas might call a complete shower. A suburban recently widowed woman is buggering along in life wholly unaided by her horrible friends, idiotic son and puerile putative daughter-in-law. An apparently dull-witted victim of circumstance thanks to a an empty post-modern script, *Mum* feels as dead as her husband.

I like my comedy coal-black, so a new genre, the pom-hom-zom-rom-com, *High & Dry* (Channel 4) was bound to grow on me. Brett Sullivan, played by writer Mark Wootton, is an Australian airline steward who has fallen for a passenger before saving his life when their flight crashes on a desert island. Other survivors turn up as he is massaging "the caviar of face-creams" into the skin of the man least likely to return his advances, but that's something that wouldn't get in Brett's way. Our loopy steward soon finds his niche as "King of the Island" and in preventing the group's rescue. Brett is as wonderfully vicious, camp creation.

The best laughs on TV have nothing to do with what is tagged as comedy. The news has always been tragi-comic but is increasingly bordering on the absurd, as society apparently concerns itself with words rather than sticks and stones. Wars are raging across the world, but someone in the Commons shouts at a staff member, or asks them out to dinner in a creepy way, and they're terribly upset about it

– headline news! Jeremy Corbyn is pro-Palestinian so *Newsnight* – it's surprising that news analysis can be so readily reduced to the ingenuous stuff of teenage social media posts – must debate whether that means he's anti-semitic. Really?

If I've become a red-faced reactionary, Donald J. Trump has long been a cartoon figure. This unfortunately takes the gilt off *Our Cartoon President* (Sky Atlantic), which does what it can to make fun of a man who does such a good job of it in person he's a tough act to follow. Nothing here is so extreme that we can't actually witness or predict any less from Trump himself. It's funny enough, but some of the White House caricatures may be lost on a British audience.

Patrick Melrose (Sky Atlantic) is the anti-heroic *alter ego* of novelist Edward St Aubyn. Even as he makes a bid to wean himself off the heavier A-class narcotics, Melrose – Benedict Cumberbatch on sparkling form – is concerned with the *perlage* of his champagne, the pastiche in his late monster-father's musical composition and the *terroir* of the heroin he aims to forgo. Child abuse aside, the histrionics are funny, the language and people refreshingly English and as authentically class-bound as television drama dares to be these days, even with period material. ☻

Astronomy

Twilight of the planets

Robert Katz scans the gloaming for a glimpse of Venus and divines a warning from our fragile universe

SUMMER days can be perfect for a little light astronomy. The amateur astronomer needs nothing but a clear sky to achieve escape velocity and leave the teeming Earth behind. After all, the day sky is just the night sky with sunlight scattered all over it. The stars and planets are still there, just washed out by the light of of the Sun. Most people have noticed the Moon during the day, even if only by accident. It looks pale and white against a blue sky, with delicate grey shadings where the great flat plains of volcanic basalt stretch for hundreds of miles on its cratered surface. Depending on the phase, you can easily spot the dark area to the right and a little bit up from the centre of Cynthia's face where earthlings Armstrong and Aldrin landed in 1969. Then it is a simple leap to imagine standing there, on the airless, bone-dry Sea of Tranquillity a quarter of a million miles away and looking out towards the Earth where it's a beautiful summer's day. Believe me, I often do.

From the surface of the Moon, the Earth is supposed to look like a blue marble with white swirls of clouds and hints of ochre, brown and green, that, if you held up your thumb, you could blot out of the pitch black sky. The idea is indeed breathtaking and sobering, but is it true? How big does the Earth look from the Moon?

An adult human thumb subtends two degrees when viewed at arm's length. The Moon in our skies is more or less half a degree wide, so we can easily blot it out with a pretty thin thumb. I tried it just now and my little finger was easily sufficient. From the Moon the Earth appears on average about two degrees wide, which is obviously four times bigger than the Moon appears to us here. But a thumb would do it – erase us all completely – especially if it is encased in an airtight space glove (which is not exactly optional attire on the Moon).

Now that you've blotted out the Earth with your thumb, or more poignantly perhaps, held our world delicately between thumb and forefinger, how are you going to feel? Terrified: like the mother of a new baby, apparently, because the Earth seems so small and helpless in the dateless night of space. Neil Armstrong though it looked like a "tiny pea, pretty and blue".

"When I first looked back at the Earth standing on the Moon, I cried," said astronaut Alan Shepard. The word Michael Collins used to describe the Earth as he orbited the Moon while Armstrong and Buzz Aldrin took in the "magnificent desolation" of the Moon's surface, was "fragile".

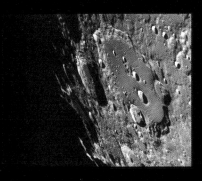

Magnificent desolation: the lunar crater Clavius, R Katz, 2016

Back on Earth, I stand in my back garden in broad daylight at the eyepiece of my laughably huge telescope peering into the blueness of the sky. What am I looking at? Certainly not the Sun: one glance with the unaided eye could damage it permanently, one blink through a telescope and your retina is toast. You *can* project the image of the Sun quite safely through a telescope onto some white card though, and the further away the card the bigger the image, which will allow you to see strangely shaped sunspots, some of them bigger than the Earth.

No, this summer I'm looking at Venus, as I always do when it crosses the sky in the south during the day far enough away from the Sun to view safely. At twilight the planet is the third brightest thing in the sky apart from the Sun and Moon and with a clear horizon you'll see her easily in the west following the direction the Sun is setting. When Galileo looked at Venus through his rudimentary telescope he discovered that she had phases like the Moon.

To us this is now banal: Venus orbits between us and the Sun, so she must show phases as sunlight illuminates her globe from various positions. To Galileo in the early 17th century it was an astrophysical and philosophical wrecking ball with which to destroy the pristine, crystalline spherical, Earth-centred universe supported by the Church. He wrote to his friend Johann Kepler in a nonsense Latin anagram which unscrambled announced the news that *Cynthia figuras aemulatur mater amorum*: "The Mother of the Loves imitates the phases of Cynthia". Venus has phases like the Moon.

Dusky Venus. R Katz, 2016

That's what I'm looking at now with my telescope as the Sun beats down; a tiny half-Moon shaped planet clothed in dazzling white clouds. I can do this because I have an "equatorial" mounting which tells me fairly accurately where the telescope is pointing using graduated circular scales on each axis. These are charmingly made of brass, but any reasonably cheap modern computer-controlled telescope will do the same job if you set it up correctly. Just remember never to point it near the Sun and if you're a beginner with Venus, definitely don't try and find her in daylight.

I have been looking at Venus with all sorts of telescopes at all times of the year, in daylight and dusk, since 1972 and she is without fail utterly disappointing. There's nothing to see. A few dusky patches of cloud formation perhaps; a brightening near the poles. The year I was born, Patrick Moore was able to sum up everything we knew about Venus in 125 pages. That amounted to practically nothing apart from the fact that the planet is surrounded by thick clouds of carbon dioxide. Earlier astronomers such as the brilliant polymath Baron Franz von Paula Gruithuisen, had plenty of theories about what was going on under those clouds.

Von Gruithuisen was lauded for inventing a treatment for gallstones, but is now (unjustly I think) ridiculed for suggesting in the 1830s that the inhabitants of Venus enjoyed a climate similar to that of Munich in the summer and lit great fires to celebrate the coronation of their Emperor.

Now we know Venus is our hellish non-identical twin: almost exactly the same size, but choking in a crushing atmosphere of smog, with a surface as hot as a furnace, turning the wrong way. A

Cytherean day is longer than a Cytherean year because the planet revolves painfully slowly in a clockwise fashion. (There is still no correct adjective for Venus as Moore pointed out in 1961 – *Venusian* is incorrect and ugly and *Venerian* is also jarring; *Cytherean* is the least bad). Plus the north pole faces so far down it's looking south. It's all wrong.

Yet Venus is a staggeringly beautiful star when seen with the naked eye before sunrise or after sunset. Have a look at dusk this month. Paradoxically dull as she is bright when you gaze at her idly through a telescope, she is also a ghastly warning from the future of what happens when global warming really starts motoring on our fragile blue pea.

Crescent Venus by Damian Peach

Travel

Lazy safari afternoons

Tim Lott kicks back like a leopard in a steampunk lodge in Sri Lanka

I'VE never been a fan of safaris. So-called "wild" animals are extremely lazy, unless they are trying to kill something. So when you've spent three or four hours trundling in a jeep through *veldt* or jungle, the chances of finding an interesting creature that is doing anything other than yawning or sleeping is fairly rare. The hope that you'll catch them chasing some smaller or weaker animal – now that's entertainment – is a long shot.

This is why you need to balance the safari experience with some high-end idling opportunities – essentially, paying tribute to the wild by loafing about just as much they do. This is why I was drawn to the Wild Coast Tented Lodge in Sri Lanka, which, even if you have

[Photo by Tim Evan-Cook]

no interest in stalking animals whatsoever, you still have the opportunity to pass the time very pleasantly.

It's located on the edge of 98,000 hectares of Yala National Park and unusually for a safari destination, is built on a beachfront. It's a "tented lodge", although it isn't really comprised of tents. It comprises pods, or cocoons (they call them "loopers" or "urchins") all built on stilts and constructed out of PVC-coated polyester. Bizarrely these spacious pods are done out in Edwardian steampunk style, all brass pipes, antique desks, leather chairs, portholes and curtained four poster beds. It's like a Jules Verne-inspired vintage train carriage. There is a brass bath with feet, rugs on hardwood floors and a large balcony outside ceiling-to-ground windows.

The pods themselves and the architecture of the communal areas are inspired by the giant red boulders, hanging wasps nests and termite mounds that are typical of the landscape in this part of Sri Lanka. It gives the property an organic, natural feel. This is added to by the adobe structures used for toilets and outbuildings.

It has a library, an infinity pool and an open-air restaurant and bar overlooking the pool. The food in the restaurant is a mixture of Sri Lankan specialties – my favourite was the egg hoppers they serve for breakfast, a kind of Dhosa with fried eggs and spices – and international cuisine. Both bar and restaurant are reminiscent of cathedrals, with bamboo simulations of organ pipes hanging over the bar space. From the outside, the roof is divided into serrated sections, and at night the artificial light glows through the gaps, creating a magical, or spaceship, atmosphere. Blue-grey outside, pink within.

Standing as it is in the middle

Photo by Tim Fryan-Cook

[Courtesy of Nomadic Resorts]

[Photo by Tim Evan-Cook]

of the jungle, you are greeted on arrival with wild pigs gathering around a water hole. Animals frequently wander in and out of the hotel grounds, among them elephants, boar and buffalo. The property is unfenced so you really are part of the wild.

The safari itself lasted about three hours and – compared with some of the experiences I have had on safari in Africa – was extremely civilised. Although the park itself can get very busy, on the day we went out, it seemed fairly quiet. That is until we spotted a leopard snoozing under a rock (there is the highest concentration of leopards in the world here). After about 30 seconds of silent observation, the first of a battalion of jeeps began to turn up (some sort of bush telegraph operates), skidding and screeching behind and in front, packed with tour groups.

We set off shortly after this, listening to our guide instruct us about the creatures existing, mostly unseen, around us. Elephants of course, but also snakes (vipers, boa constrictors, the Sri Lankan flying snake), mongooses, warthogs, a tapestry of colourful birds and the baddest of them all, the sloth bears, which apparently are the "most psychopathic bears in the world"

[Courtesy of Nomadic Resorts]

despite their cute name and cuddly appearance. They don't like humans in the slightest so I was rather hoping we didn't run into any of them.

We didn't meet any sloth bears, but we did meet some curious elephants, some with a tusk missing, which they had lost in a fight for dominance with another male. Just to gaze at this imposing creature in the wild is an excitement – slightly added to by the fact I had just watched a YouTube video of one attacking a jeep full of terrified tourists in a nearby location.

Returning to the tented camp, I necked a sundowner on the beach – a whisky sour as I recall – while the waves sent up clouds of spray behind me as they crashed on the rock. Then I relaxed into my evening meal.

The excellent meat in that night's barbecue had been killed for me, but, standing as I was at the top of the food chain, I was quite happy to leave that to others. After that I made my way back to the cocoon – watching furtively for rogue sloth bears – but made it back to a deep and pleasant sleep in a sumptuously appointed four-poster-bed. Now that's my idea getting back to nature, *Idler* style. 🐌

Rates at Wild Coast Tented Lodge start from $445 per person per night, based on two sharing, including all meals, drinks and a daily game drive.

BOOK TOWNS

FORTY-FIVE PARADISES OF THE PRINTED WORD

BY ALEX JOHNSON

PUBLISHED BY FRANCES LINCOLN · £14.99 HARDBACK

Amid the beauty of the Norwegian fjords, among the verdant green valleys of Wales, in the shadow of the Catskill Mountains and beyond, publishers and printmakers have banded together to form unique havens of literature.

Book Towns is the first directory of the best – some official members of The International Organisation of Book Towns, and others yet untitled but every bit as charming. Combining practical travel advice and illuminating histories, it's a must-have for literature-lovers and travellers the world over.

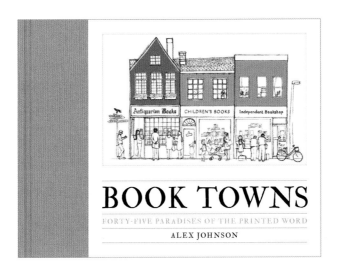

Wine

From friseur to vintner

Anne McHale *meets a hairdresser who gave it all up to make wine in Bordeaux. Photos courtesy of* **Dawn Jones-Cooper**

WHILE wine in its most basic state is just about the idlest drink there is, in practice the modern occupation of winemaker is *not* an idle one. So what prompted Dawn Jones-Cooper to move from a comfortable urban lifestyle working as a hairdresser in London to making award-winning wine from her own organic vineyard in Bordeaux?

How did you first come to own a vineyard?

My husband Jay and I had been working for many years in London, he as an independent financial advisor and me as a hairdresser. In 2005 we finished the total rebuild of our boat, a Dunkirk Little Ship called *The Gainsborough Trader* which we had been living aboard for 16 years in Surrey Quays. We wanted a new challenge and decided to look for a riverside property in Europe. We eventually settled on the Monfaucon Estate, just ten

The lure of the grape: Dawn's vineyard

minutes south of St Emilion in the Entre Deux Mers in Bordeaux. It was a bargain – you'd be hard-pressed to find a one bedroom flat in London for the same price. The estate had an old vineyard attached. In May 2006 I had signed up for a four-year, part-time degree in Viticulture and Oenology at Plumpton College in East Sussex. I realised how diseased and neglected the current vineyard was, so we decided to rip out the old vines and start again from scratch.

What have been your biggest challenges so far?
Constant commuting back and forth between the UK and France to ensure that all the work got done to a high standard while we made a living in the UK. Other challenges: living in a caravan on the estate for four years; building the vineyard from scratch; jumping through hoops in order to achieve organic certification: making our first wine on a micro budget, and a major one: losing 70% of our crop in a sudden 25-minute hailstorm in 2013. Luckily we were welcomed into our French community with enthusiasm and open arms… although the welcome was quickly followed by the friendly comment, "You know it's very important that your first wine is good, to gain the respect of the other local producers."

It doesn't sound like there is anything very idle about wine production, then…
I'm afraid not! I think we have had about 12 days off in total since 2010. The trade-off is though that you are your own boss, you are communing with nature on a daily basis and you are producing something that you can be proud of.

Tell us about your philosophy and your wines.
At Plumpton I studied organic

Fermenting away: the grapes idly turn themselves into wine

and biodynamic-based projects. The more I looked at those ways of farming, the more I decided they were the methods I wanted to follow. Our wines now have organic status (meaning that their level of sulphites is much lower than in conventional wines), and in addition my viticultural and vinification methods follow biodynamic principles. I would like to achieve biodynamic certification as only 3% of growers in the whole Aquitaine region have achieved this, but there's a way to go yet. We are also moving towards lower alcohol. Many wine drinkers are moving away from 13%+ wines; we also believe that for white wines in particular a higher alcohol content can mask the fruit flavours.

We currently produce seven still white wines and two sparklings. We believe in quality rather than quantity, pressing the grapes very gently to extract only the finest juice.

What's the story behind your catchy brand name Nobody's Perfect?
"Nobody's Perfect" as a brand name is an eye-grabber. It expresses that feeling of enjoying a naturally good wine in a relaxed and comfortable way, and in the event of quickly finding your way to the bottom of the bottle, one can easily call on that exact same expression, just as the French do with a shrug of the shoulders (*"personne n'est parfait!"*) while gleefully applying the corkscrew to a second one …

What are your plans for the future?
At Plumpton I was advised, quite rightly, to "find a niche market", and so Jay and I found inspiration in wanting to be one of the few vineyards in Bordeaux to produce sparkling wine in-house from start to finish. This is very unusual as most sparkling producers make the base wine and then allow the local syndicate to finish the rest: second fermentation, riddling, disgorging, dosage and corking. We've just released our first sparklings to great critical acclaim. We've planted a further hectare of vineyard including some red varieties, and are moving forward with plans to develop an educational experience for visitors to learn the hands-on nuts and bolts of viticulture and vinification.

In the UK you can drink Dawn's wine at four London venues; 108 Bar & Brasserie in Marylebone, The Coral Room, Dalloway Terrace in Bloomsbury, Town House in South Kensington and the esteemed wine members' club at 67 Pall Mall. You can also buy her wine through 20h33.co.uk/ and can contact her on info@chateaudemonfaucon.com.

Gin

Thrilling distilleries

Geraldine Coates goes day tripping with her favourite tipple

IF the ultimate sign of incompetence is being unable to organise a piss up in a brewery, is providing an enjoyable day out at a distillery the opposite? Possibly not and the point of visiting a distillery isn't to get drunk. No, no, no, although stories are still told, albeit in whispers, about the famous distillery that used to host a lock-in every Friday when the great and good of the town, including HM's Customs and Excise officers, would gather to drink vast quantities of the finest English gin. Those days are long gone, sadly.

Now however the good news is that, wherever you are in the UK, you won't be far from a gin visitor centre where you can discover all

A day out in a gin factory – what's not to like?

you ever needed to know. From the Hebrides to Cornwall, gin distillers are throwing open their doors and revealing their secrets.

There are many reasons for this. Gin makers have learned a thing or two from their whisky *confrères* and realise that education and knowledge are key to spreading the love and building brand loyalty. People might forget which particular gin they preferred at one of the many tastings that happen throughout the year, but they will always recall visiting the actual distillery where that gin is made.

Very often these distilleries are located in interesting, scenic places where there is a dearth of conventional tourist attractions. So the distilleries on the Isle of Harris and Shetland and other remote parts of the UK play an important social role in their communities and do a great job of boosting the local economy and providing employment.

It's also about money. Setting up a distillery is a major financial commitment and it can take some time for your gin to gain that all-important distribution deal. In the meantime, hosting tours and tastings can provide a very useful income stream. Marcus Pickering of Pickerings Gin, located in the former dog kennels of what was once the Dick Vet School in Edinburgh, now the arts centre Summerhall, explains: "About 10 % of our annual turnover is from distillery visits, not just the tours but also people buying our gin when they're here. We just won a major visitor attraction award, so that is fantastic for our profile." Not to be sniffed at.

Google "gin distilleries to visit in the UK" and you will get over 130,000 results in a matter of

Learn the secrets of Juniper juice at Pickerings

[Photos courtesy of Summerhall Distillery]

[Photo courtesy of Bombay Sapphire Distillery]

Shock and awe: Bombay Sapphire Distillery

seconds. London alone has at least ten distilleries open to the public, ranging from the majestic Beefeater Distillery in Kennington to the tiny Ginstitute in Portobello Road. The Plymouth Gin Distillery, the oldest gin distillery in the country, offers a unique opportunity to make your own gin with guidance from Master Distiller Sean Harrison. Be warned, it's not easy: my effort tasted like a blend of lavatory cleaner and cat's pee due to an unfortunately heavy hand with the coriander.

In Hampshire the Bombay Sapphire Distillery at Laverstoke Mill is total shock and awe with stunning glasshouses, designed by Thomas Heatherwick, in which some of the botanicals that go into their gin grow. The Lakes Distillery in the Lake District has won numerous prestigious tourist awards as well as accolades for its food.

I could go on but, actually, that's what the Internet is for. One thing is certain: streams of visitors to gin distilleries all over the country prove the fashionable theory that people increasingly seek out memorable experiences rather than things. Visiting a gin distillery with friends and enjoying lovely cocktails made with the spirit you've just seen being made is guaranteed to be a great day out, and, hopefully, one that you will remember.

Recipe

Get your oats

Victoria Hull *has a very easy way of preparing a great milk substitute*

If for whatever reason you have been put off dairy products, why not make your own oat milk? It's incredibly quick and cheap. Nut milks are expensive and they are costly to make at home, but oat milk costs barely anything and goes particularly well in muesli.

You may want to find alternative sources of calcium. Oats contain phytates that line your intestine and prevent calcium absorption; so commercial oat milks add extra calcium carbonate and calcium phosphate. Calcium carbonate is the lime in hard water that clogs kettles and I have plenty of that so I reckon if I eat my calcium rich dark greens, and some seeds, and carry using dairy milk in my tea, I'll be just fine.

There is a long-winded way of making oat milk – you soak the oats first, rinse them, blend them with fresh water in the proportion oats to water 1:4. Then you sieve the milk through a gauzey bag, squeezing it

through with your hands. But the idle way is below and I can't taste the difference.

Oat milk, the idle way:

1 part oats to 9 parts water
Pour oats oats into a blender, preferably a high-powered blender.
Then pour in the water.
Whizz it all up.

Drink it. Pour it onto cereal. Use it in a smoothie. Or chill it in the fridge for the next day.

It only lasts about three days but since it takes 20 seconds to make it's easy to have fresh each time. Remember to shake it, as the oat residue sinks to the bottom. ☙

Gardening

Heal thyself

Tansy
(Tanacetum
Vulgare)

A meander on the beneficial properties of herbs by **Graham Burnett**

THE healing properties of herbs have been recognised for millennia, with vast amounts of knowledge and wisdom transmitted by indigenous healers down the centuries. However the first comprehensive written record of plants of medicinal value was compiled in the fourth century BC by Hippocrates, the Greek physician known as the "Father of Medicine". When the Romans arrived in Britain almost 2000 years ago they brought with them practical knowledge in the fields of nutrition, health and medicine, and introduced many herbs grown for their health-giving properties in their monastery gardens. By the Middle Ages these had evolved into what were known as "Physick Gardens" where a variety of herbs would be cultivated. The development of printing in the 15th century saw the production of many "Herbals", magnificent books featuring descriptions and

illustrations of plants along with their healing properties and details of their preparation. Nicholas Culpepper (1616–54) was one of the best known British herbal healers. Despite his tremendous knowledge, and the fact that his *Complete Herbal* produced in 1649 is still respected today, he died penniless, accused of "witchcraft" by his more orthodox contemporary doctors due to the amazing numbers of cures he effected. Indeed, much indigenous knowledge of native herb lore was lost or suppressed by the Church during the witch hunts.

The "Doctrine Of Signatures" propounded the theory that the appearance and general characteristics of a plant gave clues as to its healing and useful properties, having been placed there as a "signature" of God. For example, lungwort (*Sticta pulmonaria*) was held to be a cure for complaints of the chest due to its spotted leaves that give the plant a resemblance to the human lung. Indeed, lungwort is mucilaginous, and is widely recognised as a treatment for pulmonary complaints. Similarly, according to the "Doctrine of Signatures", willow (*Salix spp.*) was observed to thrive in cold, wet conditions, and was thus believed to be a treatment for the rheumatic pains suffered by farmers and gardeners working outdoors in such conditions. Analysis has shown however that one active ingredient of willow bark is salicin, which, used internally, relieves and soothes the cramping fire of "the screws", and aspirin (derived from willow bark) is recommended today as one of the best remedies for chronic rheumatism.

Indeed, in the 21st century, much herb-lore that had once been held as superstition is now acknowledged as scientifically-proven fact. Radical Herbalism (radicalherbalism.org.uk) is about reclaiming and sharing knowledge of healing plants, empowering all to have the skills and ability to be able to look after themselves naturally: "We honour plant communities through conscious cultivation, ethical wildcrafting and sustainable harvesting". All of us can become radical herbalists by incorporating elements of the "physic garden" into our own gardens or allotments by growing a selection of medicinal plants in order to create our own outdoor "first aid kit". These can be administered in forms such as tisanes, infusions, decoctions, poultices or compresses, although of course it is advisable that no medicinal treatment for serious complaints using herbal cures should be undertaken without qualified supervision. The following examples are intended for information and guidance only – we are not recommending these as a replacement for conventional medicine.

Acid indigestion
Mint – drink an infusion of leaves

Bad breath
Parsley – chew leaves
Carraway – chew seeds

Colds
Yarrow – drink infusion
Horehound – make into candy

Constipation
Plantain – seeds made into
  jelly with water

Coughs
Coltsfoot – make into syrup
Horehound – make into candy
Comfrey – drink infusion of fresh
  flowers and leaves, or fresh juice
Mullein – drink infusion

Diarrhoea
Blackberry – drink decoction
  of root or leaves

Meadowsweet – drink infusion of leaves

Disinfectant
Sphagnum – sterile wound dressing
Onions – juice is mildly effective

Flatulence
Mints – drink infusion
Chamomile – drink infusion
Fennel – chew a few seeds

Headaches
Feverfew – a leaf or two each day
Chamomile – drink infusion

Hiccoughs
Mint – drink infusion or chew leaves

Indigestion
Chamomile – drink infusion
Mints – drink infusion

Insect repellent
Rue – hang bunches of herbs

in room or store clothes with moth bags
Yarrow – use in bunches or moth bags
Southernwood – use in bunches or moth bags

Insomnia
Chamomile – drink infusion
Hops – dried hops in pillow

Nausea
Lemon verbena – drink infusion
Mint – drink infusion

Warts
Greater celandine – apply juice to wart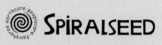

Graham Burnett is a permaculture activist and teacher, and the author of Permaculture A Beginner's Guide *and* The Vegan Book of Permaculture. *For more information on courses and publications see spiralseed.co.uk*

Beekeeping
The bee pharmacy

Plant winter-flowering blooms and cultivate mycelium while the sun is still high to make a bee's cornershop for the colder months, says **Bill Anderson**

THE plethora of midsummer pollen converging in a kaleidoscope of colours at the hive entrance on the back legs of hundreds of bees flying in as fast as others fly out to collect more can be a hypnotic sight for the idle beekeeper, sitting, watching, mesmerised by the dazzling beauty of this ballistic ballet.

While little needs to be done for the bees at this time, thousands of blossoms, many of them deliberately planted as an act of bee-friendship, are opening to provide nourishment in exchange for pollination. And there are other things we can grow to help at other times and in other ways.

Although it's difficult to imagine when the summer sun is beating down, in the winter when the bees cluster together feeding on honey to stay warm, flying any distance out of the hive to collect food can be lethal. Bees' flight muscles cannot function below 6°C, but even when

it's very cold it takes a little time for their bodies to cool down from the warmer temperature inside the hive when they fly out. Provided they're not outside in the cold for too long, they'll never cool down to the point when their wings stop working and they fall out of the sky, unable to return.

We can help them by planting winter flowering plants as close as possible to the hive, like an old-fashioned corner shop they can quickly nip out to for a few essentials, pyjamas hastily covered in an overcoat. If we plant them now, there's a good chance that Mahonia, Aconite, Winter Clematis "Wisley Cream" and Winter Honeysuckle will offer some very local pollen and nectar from December through till March.

But there's something else we can grow that will help the bees throughout the year and reap a delicious harvest for us too.

The forests in which the bees

lived in tree cavities for 15 million years would have looked very different from the ones we know today: humans now manage forests for timber, and the value of that timber is decimated by rot. So we quickly remove as much rotten wood from forests as possible to prevent it infecting our investment – healthy trees – which we harvest when they're mature but not decrepit. Before our husbandry, forests would have had a much higher proportion of naturally decaying wood, lying around as an essential part of their ecosystem, returning carbon and nutrients to the soil.

Maverick mycologist Paul Stamets also keeps bees. He noticed that a raised bed of woodchips in which he was growing King Stropharia mushrooms was being visited by his bees: with extraordinary determination they had lifted relatively enormous chips of wood to expose the intricate strands of mycelium growing below the surface. When he looked more closely he could see that the bees were sucking on little extra cellular droplets that the mycelium had exuded like beads of sweat. And they couldn't get enough of this underground fungus juice.

Stamets discovered that these droplets contain acids, enzymes and all sorts of messaging molecules: the mycelium is self-organising and self-educating – as it grows and penetrates its environment. The tips of the mycelium explore anything new or unfamiliar, and then epigenetically change themselves to find solutions to fight new toxins, or build new enzymes to digest new foods. These new solutions are then shared throughout the mycelial mat, which can extend unbroken for miles.

Messages can even be shared with other organisms: six bean plants were placed next to each other, their roots in separate pots; one plant was isolated from the other five and infested with aphids. The infested plant produced anti-aphid alkaloid chemicals to defend itself, the other five uninfested plants did not. The experiment was repeated but this time all six plants were growing in the same mycelium-rich soil. The isolated infested plant produced the anti-aphid alkaloids as before, but now so did all the other five plants that were not exposed to any aphids – the prompt to produce the aphid defence in the absence of aphids came from the mycelium.

We've known for some time that bees use fungus in their food preparation: "bee bread" is a staple – it's pollen fermented with wild yeasts and bacteria like that which we use to make sourdough, as well as fungi which all help to break down the cell walls of the pollen grains. This releases and predigests the nutrients contained within to maximise their bioavailabilty to the bees.

But Stamets discovered that the droplets his bees were so keen on were specifically and spectacularly antiviral too. They upregulated the bees' immune systems. It turns out they are significantly effective against human viruses such as HN51 influenza and herpes too.

P-coumaric acid found in the droplets is used by both us and the bees to control our detoxification pathways, but it's more essential to the bees – without it they can't detoxify, and toxins like neonicotinoids are more likely to build up to lethal levels.

This mycelium is a pharmacy the bees have relied on for 15 million years. And it's easy to grow in a shady part of your garden or a tub. Your local tree surgeon will probably be delighted to let you have a load of hardwood chips, and for less that £10 you can get a kilo of sawdust inoculated with spores of King Stropharia – enough for a bed of chips a metre square and 15cm deep. Kept moist, this bed will provide mycelium for the bees to mine for medication within months, and next spring you will begin to be able to harvest mushrooms that will keep emerging for up to three years, leaving your garden soil vastly enriched, or your tub full of the finest mushroom compost you might even mix with bee-friendly seeds and idly lob into neglected public soil to invigorate your neighbourhood with beauty and fertility…

King Stropharia mushrooms are huge, meaty, and best eaten young, cut thick and sautéed in butter. Delicious piled high on a slice of toasted sourdough.

Snooker

Johnson's Snookersauraus

Alex Johnson on the etymology of snooker slang

Silly mid off. Zugzwang. Rabona. All sports have their own barmy impenetrable lingo and snooker is no different.

So when I get in from snooker night on a Wednesday evening and my wife politely asks how it went, I just say, "Pretty well," or, more frequently, "I think that was the worst I've ever played". Because she does not want to to be subjected to the jargonic truth which is that: "What happened in the second frame was that I got a bad kick when I went into the pack and the pink wiped its feet on the knuckle before dropping and on the way back I got a nasty double kiss to take me back into baulk so I couldn't get the plant I was eying up. I almost asked for a rerack!" [sniggers].

Indeed, it's only when you stand back for a moment and think about some of these terms that you realise how little you know about how they actually got their name. I've spent nearly 40 years playing snooker, but

for the first 39 did not realise, for example, that the original term for "cannon" was *carambole*, the archaic Spanish term for star fruit, the red ball, and the name for an ancient cueball game that morphed into billiards. And while we're all familiar with baulk, how many of us can honestly say hand-on-heart that we know it comes from an Old English word for an unploughed ridge which then also became associated with the idea of an obstacle?

Of course you can always just invent your own, which is exactly what Alan McManus appears to have done while describing a particularly fine pot in the 2018 Welsh Open as a "striper". No, me neither.

By some distance, the most familiar terms of snooker speech are the numerous *bon mots* nurtured lovingly over time by the commentators who love to see balls going into the heart of the pocket and shots which are inch-perfect, reds that are out of commission and glances at the scoreboard when it's a case of the Crucible nerves. So let's get the boys on the baize as it's eyes down for some snooker bingo.

"Where's the white going?"
This constitutes about 50 per cent of John Virgo's total patter, sometimes adjusted if a colour ball creeps dangerously close to a pocket. It's so much a part of the sport now that I've seen spectators wearing T-shirts emblazoned with this catchphrase at the world championships. Also used at Wednesday Night Snooker Club as the cue ball hurtles pocketwards.

"[insert name here] is the best single ball potter in the game."
Mark Williams often gets the insert nod from the commentators, though some also go for Neil Robertson or Judd Trump to add a little variety. Frankly, if it were a question of betting the family silver on somebody making a pot, I think many non-commentators would choose Ronnie.

"[insert name here] is blessed with incredible cue power."
A "Crafty" Ken Doherty special.

"It's a very knowledgeable crowd here at the Crucible."
Thrown into the mix when some arcane stat has just been racked up or the point of snookers required has been reached. The crowd *is* pretty clued up, but since many of them wear earpieces which enable you to hear the commentators talking about said factoid, they could be entirely ignorant of baizecraft and still know when to clap gently or laugh quietly.

"And that's a bad miss!"
The best fictional piece of snooker commentary. Another favourite on Wednesday nights is the quasi-Partridgeism: "Smell my pot."

"Can you believe it?"
Dennis Taylor can't. And he's one of the nicest fellers you could ever wish to meet.

"That was careless."
A criticism of the kind of poor shot that I make about 30 times a frame. Often used in rotation with "He took his eye off the pot there".

"Exhibition shot coming up…"
One of the very few times that it's worth having a buzzy earpiece in so that you can be sure to watch a remarkable multi-cushion banana-swerving attempt instead of trying to rubberneck around the screen to see Ronnie on table two.

Meanwhile, for those of you who are reading in black and white, the pink is next to the green. 🌀

Escape

Rustout: the new burnout

Robert Wringham *learns a new managerial word – and advises on how to best avoid it*

THANKS to my tenuous association with workplace psychology, I was invited to attend a managerial conference in a corporate hotel on the sunkissed banks of the M8. It was always going to be dreadful, but I attended out of anthropological interest and also because I thought there might be some free wine to be had. There was no wine, only orange juice, but I found the strength not to tear the place to pieces.

My souvenir of the day (or my "take-home", as these managerial types strangely say) was a single word: "rustout". In contrast to the more familiar "burnout," when a wage slave's head pops from having too much to do, "rustout" is when he or she simply decays, physically and spiritually, because of boredom.

At first, it looks like just another pro-work idea. It makes me think of a *Thomas the Tank Engine* character who, not one for pulling

carriages all day long, stays in the engine shed and falls to rust. "It's train cancer, Percy," says the Fat Controller, "and wholly deserved." That is surely the intended implication of this "rustout" and apparently the word comes from a German expression that "he who rests, rusts."

But what caught my attention is the *distinction* between burnout and rustout, partly in its own right as an observation of the two ways a job might destroy the soul, but also that the managerial creed *already know about* this, its headmen perceiving two diagnosable workplace conditions.

Unfortunately, the treatments they're currently peddling leave much to be desired. The working theory is that while burnout comes from too much stress, rustout comes from too little. Give the rusting worker more to do, they say.

My own experience tells me that office rustout comes not from being unstressed but from not valuing the mission of work, full stop. It comes from knowing that no matter how you slice it, the whole thing is ultimately a waste of human life and you're only there because there's rent to pay. Boredom springs from the fact that office life doesn't – *can't* – provide spiritual rewards for a moist, creative, human brain. It's not even supposed to. It's an economic arrangement.

Under these conditions, even when you're challenged by the quantity or quality of your tasks, the challenge only exists within the meaningless confines of the Holodeck of the workplace. So how can one really escape rustout?

Don't go to work in the first place. There are many ways to avoid reporting to a job every day, some of which have been covered in previous editions of this column. Avoid jobs wherever you can as, in the modern age, they are uniformly unsatisfying. Never accept a job and you'll never experience rustout. With so much to do and experience, rustout does not happen in the real world.

If you must go to work, use your time at the desk to plot your escape. Instead of fantasising about a lottery win or a distant pension like other wage slaves, actively plot your escape. Consider self-employment, creative practice, reducing expenses and saving the difference to bring retirement radically forward; plot the steps you'd take to get such a project of the ground. A sitting position with the access to the Internet and a notepad to hand is no bad starting point for an escape attempt. The very act of finding moments at work in which to do this without the knowledge of one's supervisors will keep things interesting and help to avoid oxidation.

Work part-time. Find a way (see this column in *Idler* 53) to reduce your employment to three days instead of five. Embrace minimalism and the anti-consumerist mindset so that you can afford the reduction in income. A three-day work week is not so bad: you have the novelty of a first day in the office after a long weekend, the relief of a hump day, and then the Friday Feeling before another long weekend. The diversity of feeling along your three days and the reduction in resentment about the work's infringement upon one's life will help you to avoid becoming a rusting shed engine.

Lead a good life outside work. Harry Hill once said a bizarre thing to a heckler, a retort now famous among comedians. He said: "You say that to me now, but I know that when I get home, there's a nice roast chicken in the oven." What he meant is that he's got other stuff going on, a private treat waiting for him outside his rather silly job. It's easy to fall into a cycle of returning from work at 6pm to nothing but television and some utilitarian cookery before the desperate need to sleep. This is a considerably rust-promoting pattern and it's a life your managers and employers are perfectly happy for you to lead, regardless of any noise they like to make at conferences about reducing rustout. Defy them.

Despite learning of the condition they've dubbed "rustout," the solution proffered by office managers is to pile more work onto the bored wage slave, to find a balance between explosion and implosion. What kind of a world is that? Escape it. 🐌

Robert Wringham *is the author of* Escape Everything! (Unbound) *and two other books. He writes essays for his subscribers at* patreon.com/ newescapologist

Sheds

Moving sheds

In praise of those sturdy wooden structures that can roar down the highway at 100 mph or merely revolve at a stately pace. By **Alex Johnson**

THERE'S only one thing better than a shed, and that's a shed that moves. Shepherds' huts provide one option for those who want to manoeuvre their pride and joy at will, and many of the new breed of tiny homes are built on trailers specifically so they can be transported. And of course you can also go down the selfbuild route. Kevin Nicks' VW Passat-based motorised shed, often seen on the country's roads raising money for charity, has been officially clocked at speeds just shy of 100mph.

But most shed-owners are not looking for quite this level of mobility; something more sedate is the order of the day, so that you won't spill your tea. This is why for over a century, sheds that slowly rotate have carved out their own little niche in the shed world.

Sculptor Henry Moore had a rather nice one at his Hoglands home in Hertfordshire (sadly it's now static), and followers of the Shed of the Year competition will remember Bryan Lewis Jones' revolving masterpiece which won the Unique category in the 2016 Shed of the Year awards, narrowly missing the top overall prize.

But the most famous by far is the one owned by playwright and general all round egghead George Bernard Shaw who was inspired by his friend and neighbour, the naturalist explorer Apsley Cherry-Garrard, who had a revolving shelter in the grounds of his house nearby. Shaw wrote *Pygmalion* and *Major Barbara* in his hut at his home in Shaw's Corner, Ayot St Lawrence, near St Albans.

Built in 1906 by Stawson's, this had a revolving base which used a series of castors mounted on a circular track. It could be adjusted via a lever to improve the light inside as well as to change the view (or just for some mild exercise). Impressively high-tech for its time, in later years the hut also contained an electric heater and had a telephone connection to the house as well as an alarm clock to warn the Nobel Prize-winner when lunchtime was imminent. Shaw made quite a song and dance about how much he enjoyed the isolation his revolving hut afforded him, portraying himself as a reclusive rural sage.

One of the aspects of the Lazy Susan-style hut which attracted Shaw was its potential for improving health. In the early 20th century, the likes of Henry and Julius Caesar and Norwich-based Boulton & Paul were the titans of the summerhouse industry and made revolving models based on small Alpine chalets in Swiss tuberculosis sanatoriums. Here, TB sufferers (Shaw lost two siblings to the disease in early life) benefited from the constant flow of fresh air, as well as ready access to sunshine. These were for use in private gardens as well as hospitals in the UK, with paintwork reminiscent of muted beach hut colours.

Today, it's not easy to track down revolving sheds, although Bryan Lewis Jones has used his victorious shed as the basis for establishing 360 Creations (360creations.co.uk) which builds similarly high-quality rotating sheds and garden rooms. The leading model is the Ultimate Shed which naturally has a fully 360° revolving turntable and

features including sheep's wool insulation, copper roofing, a woodburning stove, underfloor heating and air conditioning. Another possibility is The Fourpenny Workshop (thefourpennyworkshop.co.uk) which builds and restores various shedlike structures, especially shepherds' huts. They also have experience in working on Boulton & Paul rotating summerhouses. However, your best bet is to hunt around salvage yards, where examples in a decent state of repair usually cost around £10,000.

If you're after some inspiration, you can see GBS and his hut in a video from the East Anglian Film Archive which also features an appearance from the funster Danny Kaye at eafa.org.uk/catalogue/1695 and more from British Pathé on Shaw's 90th birthday at britishpathe.com/video/g-b-s-george-bernard-shaw. There's an excellent video of Bryan's shed rotating on YouTube at bit.ly/rotatingshed. For more on buildings that move, the best book is *Revolving Architecture: A History of Buildings that Rotate, Swivel, and Pivot* by Chad Randl. 🌀

Alex Johnson runs Shedworking (shedworking.co.uk) and is a former judge of Shed of the Year. His latest book is Book Towns *(Frances Lincoln).*

George Bernard Shaw's writing shed
[Photo: Alex Johnson]

Eating out

The joy of pubs

Victoria Hull *rejects the allurements of members' establishments in favour of local boozers*

A FEW years ago, the *Idler* interviewed Terry Gilliam at members club Soho Farm House. It's part of a club chain "for creatives": you are not even allowed to wear a jacket. But over after dinner cocktails the great artist, comic and film director leant back and surveyed the room: "I can smell them," he said, "Bankers."

Members clubs are the fear-of-being-left-out fashion, but why? Certainly digital nomads can avoid solitude and meet over coffee at a club but you can do that at a pub. True there's wifi by day and cocktails by night and sometimes even roof top pools. But I don't want to strip off and power (well potter) down a boutique sized pool in front of well dressed latté sippers. And why would I choose only creatives to hang out with? And if I did choose only creatives to

hang out with how disappointed I would be when I found out they were actually bankers, without jackets on?

Worse, if there's been no confusion about the other members I might find myself in a club full of people just like me, and like Groucho Marx I have issues with that too. I want to get back to the pub.

In a pub you'll find the whole of the alcohol-drinking world. Choose an Irish pub, choose a City pub, choose your local, go for a country walk and collapse with a satisfying pint by a fire in a village pub, even choose a gastro pub: there will be a total mix of people. It's difficult to find a pompous pub.

In the last few weeks, we have found ourselves eating in two pubs and jolly good they were. After our recent beekeeping course in

The Holly Bush pub restaurant

Oxfordshire, the tutors and I went for supper in the local pub which turned out to be The Potting Shed in Crudwell. The Potting Shed must have had a good old fashioned pub name once but a few years ago it was taken over and turned into a gastro pub. It became a victim of its success when Prince William and his then girlfriend Kate were spotted there eating and "passionately embracing". For a while it was over-run by celebrity watchers. But it has now calmed down and proffers a good combination of proper pub punters and fantastic food.

There are vintage signs for dog food in the stone entrance which suggest a welcome for the *Idler* dog which proves to be the case: it's a slow dog-petting progress through a chain of stone-flagged, wood-fired, banquette-boothed drinking dens. In the dining room at the back the food is properly good restaurant food, not pub food at all. I had a chunk of grilled sea-bass with crispy skin and a sort of medley of lightly roasted tomatoes and squid on the side. Idle Beekeeper Bill Anderson had a big tasty tender pork chop and potatoes and fennel. Rather fancily I was asked what brand I wanted my gin and when I said I didn't mind, Bombay Saphire arrived with classy Fever Tree tonic. Beekeeper and artist Nicola's glass of house red wine was a large and

tasty Syrah. Now this for sure is a pub aimed at the local well-to-dos, and the food and booze is high-end but everyone else is at the bar too, and that's the way we like it.

Back in London we meet at Fenton House in Hampstead to plan for the *Idler* Festival. At the bottom of Fenton's garden is The Holly Bush pub. Like Fenton it was built at the end of the 18th century. Dr Johnson lived nearby with his wife for a while and it's thought he and Boswell must have often met at The Holly Bush. It's got all the 18th century charm you might crave after a long walk on Hampstead Heath: stone-paved floors, leather benches, cubby holes and a roaring fire. Upstairs you can eat in the old assembly room, gorgeous with chandeliers and large Georgian windows on two sides.

Martin Seymour, who runs The Holly Bush for Fullers, makes sure it feels local and supports the local community. He is treating us to lunch to discuss our festival plans. There are regulars at the bar as well as walkers and tourists eating in the cosy Coffee Room. Martin tells us the aim is to bring the food up to restaurant standard within two years. I had barley salad with chargrilled fennel and feta followed by a rather fancy cheesecake of sweet mascarpone and a crumble of ginger biscuits with mini flowers of jelly and meringue. Delicious

The Holly Bush pub, Hampstead

though. *Idler* editor Tom enthusiastically finished off a Barnsley lamb chop with smoked mushrooms, burnt shallot and *salsa verde* followed by cheese, oatcakes and quince jelly. We eye up The Holly Bush Board of pork pie, Scotch eggs, scratchings, squid, pickles and bread. Now that's good pub fare and we are looking forward it at our next festival meeting. The Holly Bush will be hosting the festival after party on Saturday 14th and idle tunes will be playing.

See you there! 🐌

The Potting Shed Pub,
Crudwell, Wiltshire,
SN16 9EW
Tel: 01666 577 833
bookings@thepottingshedpub.com

Supper for three with one main course each plus a Virgin Mary, a gin and tonic and a glass of wine was £73.81

The Holly Bush
22 Holly Mount, London
NW3 6SG
Tel: 020 7435 2892
hollybush@fullers.co.uk

Lunch for two with two courses at The Holly Bush would cost £36.

Beer

Re/make Re/fresh

Hollywood remakes are seldom as good as the originals. **Evil Gordon** *of BeerBods suggests that beer might have something to do with it*

"THEY'VE remade *Point Break*! When did that happen?"

Not words that I am accustomed to saying out loud but ones which formed the basis of a rhetorical question aimed at my wife one Saturday evening. At this point I realised we were really going to struggle to find something genuinely worth watching. We were also resigned to find out what kind of reboot was needed for Kathryn Bigelow's 1991 cops-and-robbers surf action movie.

It turns out that the remake was even worse than feared. So bad, in fact, that I resorted to looking out for beers subtly or otherwise featured as product placement. Yes, I realise that sounds a bit geeky but it's a game I play when a film really isn't keeping my attention.

This got me thinking. If you are going to remake a film, especially if you are going to do it badly, then you should make sure that the beer featured in it is better than the one

in the original. Then, even if your remake is poor, at least you'll be helping people to drink better beer through some clever advertising.

So this column is for any of you aspiring Hollywood director types (I know that that's exactly the *Idler* target audience despite what Tom tells me). Here are some films that seem to have escaped a 21st Century reboot this far. More importantly these are the beers you should consider including in your summer blockbuster.

Bullitt (1968):
Hitachino Nest Amber Ale
I simply cannot believe that no one has remade *Bullitt*. Even more so as this classic action thriller turns 50 this year. This film has it all and by all I mean that it has a great bad guy, a really good, good guy, a car chase to end all car chases and an

amazing soundtrack. Beer also makes an appearance. With the exception of Milwaukee-based Schlitz, the beers or beer signs that you see are Carta Blanca and Kirin which are imports from Mexico and Japan respectively. Imported beer it is then. In my reimagined version of this film we would see neon signs for Pacifica Clara (the most drinkable *cerveza* you can actually find in the UK) and, offing on the Japanese import, Hitachino Nest. I can just see the little neon owl logo glowing in the window of the *bodega* where our protagonist stops to buy a carryout of six bottles of their version of an equally classic amber ale. We can all get behind the cop who drives a Ford Mustang, listens to jazz and drinks good beer.

Dirty Dancing (1987):
Oscar Blues Mama's Little Yella Pils
"Nobody puts Baby in the corner" and it seems nobody wants to remake Jennifer Grey and Patrick Swayze's finest moments in *Dirty Dancing*. Dating back to 1987 it seems that no one makes films like this any more (rom-dram-dance?). At least that is something to be grateful for.

Throughout the film you can spot old Saranac Utica Club, Miller and Pabst signs. I'd urge you to give these beers a wide berth. With the exception, that is, of Pabst Blue Ribbon. Everyone should try this beer, even if it is just to realise that the hip kids don't always know what they are doing. Made cool again by an ironic brigade of trendsetters, this beer is surprisingly popular in craft beer circles. Less surprising is that this beer is, well, really rather bland. If you want a good, light, all-American Pilsner then Mama's Little Yella Pils by Oscar Blues Brewery in Colorado is for you. By the pioneers of canning great beer you can now get this quite easily in the UK. Did I mention that it's a great beer? No one puts this lager in the corner.

Jaws (1975):
Narragansett Fresh Catch
In Peter Biskind's controversial book, *Easy Riders, Raging Bulls* he lays blame on *Jaws* being such a big box office hit in 1975 that it consequently led to the demise of arthouse films being made in Hollywood. All the movie moguls wanted another blockbuster after *Jaws*. I'm exaggerating a bit but you get my point. You certainly can't argue against this if you've seen *Jaws* 2 and the less we talk about *Jaws* 3 the better for all concerned.

It seems that even the animatronic shark at Florida's Universal Studios couldn't inspire anyone to take on the challenge of

remaking this iconic horror. Which is a real shame because the Narragansett Brewery, whose cans feature in the original, are still going strong. It's hard to think of a beer better suited to this film than one made by this Rhode Island-based brewery – who, despite some dark times in the 1980s and 1990s, have made an astonishing comeback and embrace their cameo appearance in this film. Their hoppy golden ale, aptly titled Fresh Catch is a tribute to the men and women of New England who make their living through the fishing industry. I think Messrs Shaw, Dreyfus and Scheider would have approved. And probably needed a bigger boat.

E.T. (1982):
Modern Times Fruitlands
If Spielberg frightened us all out of the water with *Jaws*, he made us cry over a wrinkled alien life-form, left stranded on Earth by his cohorts whilst on an interstellar horticultural trip. Apart from a fab chase scene involving bunch of kids on BMXs, my favourite scene in *E.T.* has to be when our eponymous hero raids the fridge of his human

hosts and proceeds to drink a six-pack of Coors. Even, with my "Please drink responsibly" hat on and set at an ironic angle I could not recommend that anyone try to replicate this stunt. Well, not without it being a substantially better beer. In my remake I would have our interplanetary visitor chug on Fruitlands by Modern Times from San Diego. This funky, sour and slightly salty gose is seriously fruity and very, very moreish. So much so that you need some serious willpower to leave a can in your fridge. Just go easy doing any stunts on your BMX or trying to operate a Speak and Spell if you've had a can or three of this mighty fine beer.

Stand by Me (1986):
Rogue Dead Guy Ale
You'd expect something more than a Bud or Coors in Rob Reiner's *Stand By Me* and you aren't disappointed. Based on *The Body* by Stephen King, this is a classic coming-of-age drama set in small town Oregon. From Kiefer Sutherland as the archetypal bad boy to a underdog who will ultimately make good played by the late River Phoenix, this film has a lot going for it even though it is

over 30 years old. Unlike a lot of 1980s movies some more diverse beers make an appearance here. Like Ranier and (again) Pabst. Maybe this film predicts how big craft beer will ultimately become in the Pacific Northwest? I don't know who would be cast as Gordie Lachance in my better beer remake but the choice of beer would be an equally tough casting decision. There are so many great, tiny brewers in Oregon right now but my heart tells me this one should be Rogue's Dead Guy Ale (apt name). Brewed in Oregon and using hops from Rogue's own farms,

this big beer is more likely to be a tribute to The Grateful Dead than it is to be about a film about a bunch of kids who go looking for a dead body. This is Rogue's take on a German Maibock, a strong dark lager with a lot of, er, body.

Now to paraphrase the obligatory chubby kid, Vern Tessio; "If I could only have one beer to drink for the rest of my life?"

"That's easy, Dead Guy Ale. No question about it."

Come on Hollywood, even if you can't come up with fresh ideas for films you can add some fresh beers to the credits. ☺

Ukulele
Shaw thing

Cameron Murray *meets a uke legend*

MODESTLY dubbed the "King of the Ukulele", Ralph Shaw is one of the originals – a pre-Internet star who honed his craft in front of dubious, bemused audiences in the early 1990s.

"No-one around me was playing ukulele and the novelty value was powerful," Ralph admits. "Kids loved it, as did older people whose only previous exposure to the instrument was either Tiny Tim or George Formby. Simply taking the uke out of its case was enough to spark expectant laughter."

Laughter was something Ralph already knew about from his time as a clown and children's entertainer.

"In my mid-twenties, I was wondering what to do with my life when I discovered the book *The Independent Entertainer: How to be a Successful Clown, Juggler, Mime, Magician, or Puppeteer* by Happy Jack Feder," he reveals. "It was a light-bulb moment for me as I realised the possibility of living an independent life, free from the shackles of grinding employment. I later learnt that cash-free free time can be as bad as working full-time, so now I try to avoid both situations."

Originally from Yorkshire,

Ralph made a name for himself in Canada, where he founded the Vancouver Ukulele Circle. The club is celebrating its 18th anniversary this year and is the oldest in the country.

"For a long time, I was the only ukulele act in a metropolitan area of about three million," he says. "But now other classes have started and people are doing their own thing, and that's how it should be."

In 2003, Ralph released the landmark tutorial video *The Complete Ukulele Course*, which I promptly bought.

"The title pays homage to the 1653 book *The Compleat Angler* by Izaak Walton – the first how-to book ever written," he explains. "Obviously, it's not 'complete' in the sense that it shows everything you can possibly do on a ukulele, but when released it was the only video that took people beyond basic strumming and opened their eyes to many other techniques."

It was 2012 when I finally met Ralph. We were both on the bill at the Melbourne Ukulele Festival in Australia and enjoyed a few pints and a bit of a jam in the autumnal sunshine.

"My favourite memories come from the people I meet along the way," Ralph says of his travels. "I'm not a big-budget act, so I rarely stay in fancy hotels. It's always a delight to get to know the folks who volunteer to bring me into their homes. We get to know each other pretty well and I'm amazed by the interests, talents and depths of personality I discover."

Ralph has so far written two excellent books, *The Ukulele Entertainer: Powerful Pointers for Players and Performers* and *The Art of Ukulele*, in which he gets delightfully philosophical.

"There is beauty all around us, all the time. But you have to seek it out. Slow down and look carefully," he writes in *The Ukulele Entertainer*. "When you pick up your instrument and start to play, you too need to focus on the beauty. It's impossible to make true music any other way."

For almost 30 years, Ralph has stayed true to his vision and to himself as he's forged an enviable career as both a performer and teacher.

"Many years ago, the Harmony Company produced a ukulele on which was inscribed: "Music self-played is happiness self-made." That sentiment is as true now as it was in the 1920s," he says. "I don't encourage you to quit your day job without good reason. But if you have a dream, plus a tendency towards creative self-delusion, then start planning now. It's later than you think."

All hail the King!

Ukulele

Relative Poverty

Will Hodgkinson *and* **Danny Wootton** *teaches us a great song by the legendary* **Lawrence**

THE single-monicker cult star Lawrence began his career with the 1980s indie pioneers Felt: ten tasteful, dreamlike albums and ten singles in ten years, and a goal to be the greatest band of all time. It didn't happen, but then, Lawrence's eccentricities didn't help matters. He sacked his first drummer for having curly hair.

Then he took an about-turn with Denim, a pre-Britpop riot of 1970s nostalgia and pop art irony with chart appeal in mind. When that failed too, Lawrence fell down a hole of despair and never came out. The result is Go-Kart Mozart, the world's first "B-sides only" band, and *Relative Poverty*. It is really very catchy.

(F) I'm living in (A7) relative (D) poverty (D7)
(Bb) I'm living on a (C) tenner a day
(Bb) Goodness gracious
A (C) tenner a (F) day (Bb) (F) (C)

(F) I'm living in (A7) relative (D) poverty (D7)
(Bb) I'm living on a (C) tenner a day
(Bb) Goodness gracious
A (C) tenner a day

(F) I'm living in (A7) relative (D) poverty (D7)
(Bb) A-wop-bop-a-loo-la
A (C) tenner a (F) day (Bb) (F) (C)

(F) Take a look in shop doorways
(A7) Curled up on the floor

(Bb) You'll see men with no future
(F) They were wiped out in the war
(C) (A-well-u well-u well-u)

The (F) British top brass
(A7) won't do bugger all
(Bb) I don't know what's going
(F) on any (C) more

(F) I'm living in (A7) relative (D) poverty (D7)
(Bb) A-wop-bop-a-loo-la
A (C) tenner a (F) day (Bb) (F) (C)

(*Instrumental*)
F A7 Bb F C x 2

(F) He's living in (A7) relative (D) poverty (D7)
(Bb) He's living on a (C) tenner a day
(Bb) Goodness gracious
A (C) tenner a day

(F) He's living in (A7) relative (D) poverty (D7)
(Bb) Goodness gracious
A (C) tenner
(Bb) A-wop-bop-a-loo-la
A (C) tenner
(Bb) Please don't take my (C) tenner (F) away 🐚

Idler questionnaire
Ali Smith

Ali Smith's latest book, Winter, *was recently up for the Man Booker Prize. She is the author of many novels, including* How To Be Both, Hotel World *and* Artful. Winter *is the second in a quatrology of seasonal novels.*

Tell us about your new book.
Not till I've written it.

What are you reading?
The new Michael Ondaatje novel, *Warlight*. I'm an Ondaatje fan.

What was your worst ever job?
Clearing tables in Littlewoods restaurant in Inverness. I got promoted, though, to Hotplate, pretty soon, and I liked that better. There was good camaraderie; all the older women looked out for the younger ones – it was a fine place to work. But after a day clearing tables you could peel the stuck food off the soles of your shoes in the shape of little shoe-platforms.

How many hours do you work each day?
As many as I can.

Town mouse or country mouse?
Greek or Italian holiday mouse.

Does love bring happiness or unhappiness?
Yes.

Digital or analogue?
Luddite.

What are your three greatest pleasures?
Good weather, deckchair, reading.

Do you believe in the nap?
It definitely exists.

What would the current you say to the teenage you?
It'll be fine. Stop worrying. (Wry smile.)

Any message for aspiring idlers?
Casa Delfino in Chania, Crete, has a great room with a balcony overlooking the port, and is only two minutes away from Tamam, where the food is exemplary.

Whither bohemia?
Absolutely. It's the whithering height.